Healing an Angry Heart

Healing

an *Angry*

Heart

Finding Solace in a Hostile World

Cardwell C. Nuckols, Ph.D.
Bill Chickering

Health Communications, Inc.
Deerfield Beach, Florida
www.hci-online.com

Library of Congress Cataloging-in-Publication Data

Nuckols, Cardwell C.
    Healing an angry heart: finding solace in a hostile world /
Cardwell C. Nuckols, Bill Chickering.
        p.   cm.
    ISBN 1-55874-517-3 (pbk.)
    1. Anger.   2. Anger—Case studies.   I. Chickering, Bill.   II. Title
BF575.A5N75   1998
152.4'7—dc21   98-3079
                                                                  CIP

©1998 Cardwell C. Nuckols and Bill Chickering

ISBN 1-55874-517-3

Publisher: Health Communications, Inc.
            3201 S.W. 15th Street
            Deerfield Beach, FL 33442-8190

Cover design by Lawna Patterson Oldfield

To my son, Camden.
You have blessed me beyond measure.

—C. C. NUCKOLS

For Joey, my goddess in residence.
Now and Forever.
And for Midge.

—BILL CHICKERING

*Without wishing it, we human beings
are placed in situations in which the great
"principles" entangle us in something, and
God leaves it to us to find a way out.*

—C. G. JUNG

*I have learned through bitter
experience the one supreme lesson: to
conserve my anger, and, as heat conserved
can be transmitted into energy, even
so our anger controlled can be
transformed into a power which
can change the world.*

—MOHANDAS GANDHI

Contents

C. C.'s Acknowledgments xiii

Bill's Acknowledgments xv

Prologue xvii

SECTION ONE: ANGER ALL AROUND US

Chapter One: Everyday Anger

- Chapter Introduction 3
- Fishing 14
- The String 15
- Guy's Story: The Bad News—The Good News 16
- Steve's Story 23
- Take Your Technology and 28
- Verbal Abuse 32

Chapter Two: On the Road to Somewhere

- Chapter Introduction 35
- Topsy-Turvy 47
- The Neighborhood Bully... 48
- Clay's Story: The Road to Graduate School 50
- Road Rage 53
- It's Never Sweet 56

- Alan's Story 59
- You Can Keep Your Damn Anger! 64
- Henri 66

Section One Close: Managing Anger Along the Way......... 68

SECTION TWO: DEEPER HURTS

Chapter Three: Lost and Found
- Chapter Introduction..................... 83
- Where Do You Shine? 93
- One More Surprise 94
- John T. and Bryan's Story 96
- How Many Tears? 106
- Martha's Story 107
- Those Who Sustain Me 115
- Tim's Story 122
- Alice's Story 130
- Fishermen 137
- Deborah's Story 139

Chapter Four: Trusting the Process
- Chapter Introduction................. 147
- The Path................. 155
- Losing a Child................. 156
- Stand Back................. 159
- Live-In................. 160
- Richard's Story................. 161
- Digging Deep 170
- John W.'s Story 173
- Island Hopping................. 178

Chapter Five: Lessons

- Chapter Introduction 181
- Catch Me If You Can 188
- Diane's Story 189
- The Loss of a Dream 191
- Some Questions 193
- Patience 194
- Like the Poet 197
- Faye's Story 198
- The Night of Stars 203
- A Handful of Dust 206
- Steps 210

Section Two Close: Healing Never Ends 211

Epilogue 221
Works Cited 227

C. C.'s Acknowledgments

I would like to acknowledge the friendship and the contribution of stories by Walk Jones, Tom Nawrocki, John Walters and Pat Fields.

And Mickey the Cat (named after Mickey Mantle, my childhood hero).

Bill's Acknowledgments

I want to thank the courageous people who so freely told their stories for this book. I know it wasn't easy. You have my gratitude and respect.

Thanks to my nephew, John Thacker. Your story about you and Bryan got this whole project rolling. Your courage and honesty kept me on track and focused.

My family supported and sustained me during some hard times that I encountered during the writing of this book. Thank you for caring so much.

Grateful acknowledgment also to my career mentor, Barry McLeish, and my creative mentor, Ron Wilson. The kid's turned out okay, I think.

My gratitude to Chris McCarty, Scott Edelstein and Doug Toft for keeping the Zen focused and my feet on terra firma.

And most importantly, I want to thank my wife Joey for her love, her laughter, her strength and her compassion. I love you and I know with all my heart that God was beaming the day he sent me to you.

Prologue

We hope this book will speak to your heart; that it will in some way touch you where you live. If it does, we will consider it successful.

In his Nobel Prize acceptance speech, William Faulkner said that unless we write from the heart, we do nothing that is truly lasting; to reach one another we must rid ourselves of fear and rediscover the universal truths: "love and honor, pity and pride, compassion and sacrifice." We must learn, he continued, that the only thing really "worth writing about, worth the agony and the sweat" are the "problems of the human heart in conflict with itself."

The stories in this book come from hearts in conflict. The more we read them and spoke with the people involved, the more we were humbled. The people who speak in these pages allowed their anger to show. As we transcribed their tapes, we heard their crying; we heard their anger and pain being relived all over again.

There were others who tried to tell their story but after many fits and starts found they could not. Their anger was too deep. They just couldn't dredge it up again. These stories, left unwritten, also touched us deeply. We've also included some personal essays; some of our own reflections on healing that has occurred in our lives.

We've divided this book into two sections. The first section, "Anger All Around Us," speaks to the everyday irritations—some major, some minor—that frustrate and complicate our lives every day. Maybe it's an impossible boss, an inability to keep pace with technology, or dealing with angry drivers on the freeway: Whatever your source of irritation, you'll find something familiar in these stories.

The second section, "Deeper Hurts," deals with devastating, life-altering issues. You'll read stories about grief over the death of a close friend, the death of a child, sexual abuse, and recovery from addiction. These first-hand accounts of trauma and survival are moving examples of the strength of the human spirit.

Both of these sections acknowledge the journey of life; that healing takes time, and more often than not, a healthy dose of patience. The stories teach that anger is a tool that can eventually move us to the right place, even if it seems destructive and void of meaning at first.

If you're looking for a book that could be titled *Ten Steps to Get Rid of Your Anger,* this is not it. We offer no such remedies, no instant cures or magic elixirs. We don't offer them because they don't exist.

What we do offer is an honest look at life and how anger plays a part in it. No one in these stories has it figured out. In some people, anger is still very visible. Others will always be scarred, because that's often what life leaves us on the road to healing. There will always be struggle. For some the future is clear; for others it looks dim; for the rest, it appears uncertain.

These stories are not all wrapped up and neatly packaged. You're smart enough (from your own experience) to know life doesn't always work that way. Recovery from sexual abuse and incest doesn't come about in a few hour-long counseling sessions. Watching your best friend die a prolonged death is an image you'll live with forever. Working through the loss of self-esteem and life purpose that result from being unceremoniously dismissed in a corporate downsizing takes more than a refresher course in positive thinking. Living with the memory of lying next to your dying child takes more than a seminar on the stages of grief.

As we began this book, we wondered whether we would get volunteers to share their stories. That worry was dispelled rather quickly. Many of those whom we invited to contribute stories said something to the effect of, "You want angry? I'll give you angry!" And they did. Through the people in this book, we want to shine a small spotlight into your world. It is our hope that you will be able to see yourselves in these stories. If you feel alone with your problems and your anger at life, it's our wish that you will respond to some of these stories with, "Yes, that's me!"

The pain of our anger is often lifted by the story of another. It's amazing how a few points of identification can lighten our burden. Stories are powerful tools for healing. The sound of another human voice, whether spoken or heard through print, can touch our heart in a way nothing else can. It can reach way down inside to that part of us we call soul or spirit.

Healing an Angry Heart is a book about the spirit. The stories in this book are about the journeys of the heart and soul as they move toward recovery and fullness of life. While some of the people in these stories have regained their equilibrium to move about fairly well in the world, their spirit still wanders—restless and disturbed.

Others you will read about are closer to home. They still have questions; maybe they'll always have questions. But they've reached a point of acceptance; and they understand that some of their prayers and questions may never be answered.

We want these stories to motivate you to consider the role that anger has played in your life. We want this book to give you hope, and the courage and conviction you need to press on and keep your faith even when the signs seem to say no.

We hope this book will serve as a companion to you when necessary, something to lean on for strength when you need it. Whether you're going through a rough time or a time of joy, we hope you'll be able to open this book and find a friend or two waiting inside.

Finally, it's our wish that these stories will inspire you to renew and refresh yourself spiritually. As you read accounts by people who have endured and prevailed in the midst of betrayal and loss, we hope to provide you with the tools to fight the inner battle of the human heart and choose the path of the spirit over the path of fear.

SECTION ONE

Anger All Around Us

1

Everyday Anger

INTRODUCTION

The Spanish philosopher Juan Luis Vives (1492-1540) is considered by many to be the father of modern psychiatry. One of Vives's contributions was his description of the soul's functions. In his book *De Anima et Vita* (*On the Soul and Life*), he describes the body's five senses, the general mental functions and the "affects." The affects, or emotions, are divided into three groups. The first group deals with the positive emotions and includes love, desire, goodwill, sympathy, joy and pleasure. The second group includes fear, hope, shame and other emotions. In this chapter, we focus on the third group: the negative emotions of displeasure, anger, hatred, envy, jealousy and contempt.

In 50 A.D. Seneca said this about anger: "We are here to encounter the most outrageous, brutal, dangerous and intractable of all passions; the most loathsome and unmannerly; nay, the most ridiculous, too; and the subduing of this monster will do a great deal toward the establishment of human peace." Seneca, like Vives, views anger from a negative perspective.

Maybe anger has been given a bad rap. Could there be another side to this most vivid of all emotions? Before we look into the positive aspects of anger, let's inspect its darker side, for certainly the negative reputation of anger and its resulting acts of aggression is merited.

Just turn on the television. Somebody does something bad. A hero gets indignant and is righteously enraged. Somebody pays for this, and we applaud. Even the cartoons of our youth were full of anger and aggression. Remember Popeye and Bluto? They constantly fought, and although no one was ever killed, each cartoon was filled with escalating acts of violence as Popeye and Bluto fought for that love goddess, Olive Oyl.

In the newspapers we read daily of angry comments and threats of retaliation. If it's not Castro making an angry remark directed against American democracy, it's some madman threatening to blow up the world if his demands are not met.

Acts of violence surround us. There certainly is wickedness in the world. As Dr. Saul Levine graphically states, "It abounds, it surrounds us, it is as integral a part of our life experience as are love and loss. Who has not been perturbed and affected in the course of their lives by the wanton wickedness and iniquity inherent in others? Always others. We are fascinated, and of course, appalled by the malignity of mankind. The public is preoccupied with the evil acts perpetrated by iniquitous individuals and groups. We read about evil in our newspapers, hear about it on the airwaves and watch it on television, and movies. We do all of this avidly, and, as media executives well know—evil sells! No fools they: evil and viciousness are prevalent and popular, ubiquitous and universal, endemic and indigenous. It was always thus, it will always be. . . ."

Wander through a neighborhood in the lower socio-economic part of any city. Look around you and remember the way you grew up. Now observe the gang graffiti. Hear on the news about drive-by shootings. Read the literature on physical, sexual, and emotional abuse perpetrated on children. Over time watch the effects. These children begin to feel that there is no future for them. This has been described as terminal thinking. We used to think that this occurred only in areas of the world that were war zones, but a very similar phenomenon is occurring in children growing up in violent areas in America. Ask some preteens and adolescents about their future. Ask them what they plan to do when they grow up, and you may get a shocking reply. They might say that they don't think about the future; that they don't believe they have a future and don't expect to live past the age of twenty.

Anger is not one-dimensional. It is not easily understood. There is no one cause; there is no one solution. First it's important to make a distinction between anger and aggression. Anger is a subjective feeling, and associated with this feeling are certain thought processes, physiological processes and arousal patterns. Aggression, on the other hand, is a behavior. It is intended to do harm or injury to a person or object.

Anger can be seen through two sets of glasses. We can see it as a symptom of an underlying psychological or psychiatric problem, or as a learned survival skill—a way to deal with an environment that is perceived as hostile.

Some people have psychological or psychiatric problems of which anger is a manifestation. For example, some people with seizure disorder may experience anger before, during or after the ictal, or seizure state. Some persons who have experienced head trauma may lose some ability to control their emotions; thus their anger can be exaggerated. Physical conditions such as tumors in the brain can also cause angry outbursts. An example of this is evident in the case of Charles Whitman, who, from a tower at the University of Texas, shot randomly at crowds of people. Physicians discovered a tumor the size of a walnut infringing on the amygdala in his brain. Some people suffer from personality disorder. These people see the world in a different way. We all remember the bombing of the federal building in Oklahoma City—a classic case of anger turned into aggression. This anger was generated from the perpetrators' paranoid view that the world was, in some way, out to get them. Shortly after the bombing, Timothy McVeigh was pulled over by a police officer because he didn't have a license tag on his pickup truck. When the officer asked him why he did not have the license tag, McVeigh's response was, "because I fear government invasion." He had just planned an almost perfect crime, having spent months to years in the process, but he refused to put a license tag on his getaway truck. This is extreme paranoid thinking.

Certainly anger can be seen as evil. In our world there are people who are antisocial. Their antisocial behavior plays out in many ways. Some hide behind religion like David Koresh and Jim Jones; others display antisocial behavior and narcissism by initiating hostile takeovers. It is not just murderers and robbers who hurt those around them. In a way this can be fairly easily understood. Many feel that genetics are involved in the development of this malevolent antisocial behavior. From a religious perspective we may describe the biblical fall of man as the time when evil entered the world. From an evolutionary perspective the survival of the fittest determines who lives to produce the next generation. Certainly from a Darwinian point of view there is some merit in hitting first. For those of us in America, just think about how this country started. The Europeans and others migrated to America because they could not live with the government restrictions in the country in which they abided. They did not want to live in countries where they were told what to do and how to do it. Certainly there were some antisocial traits among these individuals, and all of this was brought into the melting pot we now call America.

Anger can also be seen from a contextual perspective, on which this book is based. The stories contained herein are not about people with diseases or disorders, but people who respond to life situations with anger and rage. Sometimes the anger and rage are appropriate; sometimes they are not. There is always a lesson to be learned somewhere.

Anger is all around us. Look at the changes in our communities within the last three or four decades. When many of us were growing up, there were always family members around to teach and help us. If a family member wasn't available there were usually neighbors and other community members to help. Today, children and adolescents are expected to accomplish more, but with less support than before. Unfortunately, their self-expression has taken precedence over their discipline, and their self-centeredness has taken the place of their participation in the community.

For many, extended families no longer exist. Every Sunday, when I was growing up, we all spent the day with each other after church: the dogs, the cats, the aunts, the uncles, the grand-parents and the cousins. The family portrait of today for so many is so different.

It can be a cold and mechanical world with high tech and low touch. In the story "Take Your Technology and . . ." you'll read about a young man who works by himself in his office all day. His only relationship is with his computer. He communicates to others not by manuscripts, meetings or phone calls, but via computer disks. He rarely experiences a handshake or receives a smile. There is often very little negotiation between this writer and his assistant editor. All communication from the authors is by computer disks. This is the medium of communication. If historically this had been true, we would probably lack most of the great literature we have today. Do you really think Hemingway and Faulkner would have put up with this? This short piece speaks to the anger and frustration experienced by someone who feels misunderstood because he cannot communicate with human beings. It is all so mechanical and at times so very cold.

Many of us experience the same phenomenon in our daily lives. We may talk to dozens of people on the phone, receive numerous faxes, but we do not look anyone in the eye. There is no handshake or parting smile of understanding. We are just left holding the phone and wondering whether we were understood.

We learn at an early age to make important decisions in an effort to manage the anger around us. This is especially true if we grow up in an environment devoid of loving, caring and support, a community beset with violence, gangs and drugs or in a neighborhood that lacks the ability to nurture a child. We learn, generally between the ages of eight and eighteen, to make decisions that may include never letting anyone get close to us again in order to never let anyone hurt us again. Our experience with others, especially adults, may be negative. Because we are neglected or hurt, or because of what is happening around us, we choose not to participate. Obviously, this affects us as we grow older and have to hold jobs, maintain relationships, raise kids and develop a family. Anger is a protective device we use to keep people away. No one wants to get close to someone who is angry. We may remember the angry experiences of our youth, and because of that, we distance ourselves from situations where anger exists to avoid experiencing anxiety and other subjective distress. This is the way we learn to cope and survive. Unfortunately, when we use anger as a means to distance ourselves from others, we also drive away those who wish to help us.

It's much easier to understand anger than to change it and reduce the behavior that results from it. Simple formulas don't work. There are no ten steps to make your anger go away. You are angry because you are. It's rather existential when you pause to think about it. Yes, there are ways to understand your anger. There are even ways to help reduce the problems caused by the anger. Never become deluded into thinking that you can just make your history and your anger disappear. If you remember the old *Bob Newhart Show* in which Bob was a psychologist, you probably recall the character Mr. Carlin. That guy must have worked with his anger for at least ten years, yet it never seemed to go away.

Maybe the way we look at anger is not appropriate. What if we step back a little and observe anger not as negative, but as potentially positive energy? What if we view it as something we learned that helped us out? Then we really wouldn't want to make it go away. There are times when anger is very useful. There are times when anger sends a very clear message to others.

There are also times when anger is used for power and control, to establish dominance over another person or to put another in a "one-down" position. This multidimensional, misunderstood emotion might best be seen in regard to its potential to teach us about ourselves. Certainly, when we feel anger, our bodies and minds are telling us to pay attention and look at what is going on around us. There is potential learning in this experience.

In "The String" we explore a general judgment of a person displaying anger as someone who is incomplete or lacking in problem-solving skills. This story helps us to understand that all of the emotions are part of what makes us special and unique. It also reminds us that often our anger builds, and minor issues are generalized and blown out of proportion. Very rarely do things turn out as badly as we have imagined. Our lack of emotional control combined with our cognitive ability to fabricate excessive outcomes to minor situations creates a feeling of loss of control, which increases our anxiety, fear and potential anger.

Maybe there is a lesson in our anger. Maybe it is not to be avoided. It might be best just to step back from it, take a few breaths, and consider its source and the lesson that might be learned.

Existence and anger seem inseparable. In "Guy's Story: The Bad News—The Good News," the existential issue is addressed as follows: "Ultimately the truth is that each of us is angry by the fact that we exist physically in the world." The story goes on to illustrate that conflict, frustration and anger are all part of the bargain of being alive. Don't be afraid of anger. It gives us valuable information about others and ourselves. Give anger space to be heard. Use those you trust as sounding boards. Realize that anger can ultimately teach us valuable lessons. Worldviews can change, as can one's essence.

In "Guy's Story" Guy learns, with both surprise and fear, just how explosive his anger can be, and how anger can spew forth uncontrollably to hurt and wound. That's the downside of anger. But he speaks of the upside as well, and talks freely and openly about how anger is often a very strong cue that something in our life needs immediate attention.

Guy speaks of anger that is understandable and justifiable: anger against those who rape, abuse children or are prejudiced, or against any sort of blatantly unjust or willful malicious act against another. The anger that perplexes him is the anger that comes out of nowhere, the anger that occurs between two people who have lifetimes of pent-up rage that can erupt at any moment. It is true that in a relationship we bring all the history of both families into the picture. It is also true that we learn so easily how to push each other's buttons. This gives us a certain power, but this power can inhibit the growth of the relationship. It's only when this anger is looked at, stepped back from and understood that it creates energy for growth within the relationship. It tells each partner that something desperately needs attention.

In a similar manner, the story "Fishing" speaks to the issue of acting out anger within the family. In this small portrait you will observe a father dealing with his son's expression of anger after the child has viewed a violent program on television. It is not the anger that is a problem, because in this house anger can be expressed openly. It is the son's acting out that is not okay. Earlier we noted that in many kids today self-expression is valued over discipline. But they're often taught discipline nonetheless. In "Fishing" we'll see that the father employs a disciplinary measure because of his son's violent acting-out episode. But, like many measures instituted in the home, this one didn't turn out as planned. In this story, a five-year-old loses his fishing privileges but, through the creativity possessed only by a child, finds a way to fish without his Mickey Mouse pole. The important point of the story is not so much the child's creativity as it is the father's statement that violence and acting-out behaviors are not okay. Mothers and fathers, in situations like this, can only hope the child understands that lesson. It is not certain whether the lesson learned by the child is about the inappropriateness of acting out or about getting punished and finding a way around it, or both.

Maybe there is another lesson to be learned from anger. If left unchecked, anger can consume you. It can create havoc and disrupt focus. It can limit one's ability to interface effectively with one's family and friends. As a matter of fact, anger can totally immobilize you. Take "Steve's Story" for example. After twenty-four years of service—loyal service—his dreams were shattered. At fifty-five, Steve is laid off. It is called "downsizing," but to the employee it is a disruption of self-concept and the ability to provide.

Steve is distracted, depressed and full of stuffed rage. His wife wants him to seek counseling. Steve just doesn't seem to be there anymore. Further diminishing his self-concept is his decision to take a job that pays only half what he had been earning as a middle manager. With a child going to college, and after already having dipped into his pension fund, Steve saw no alternative. He had to take a position for much less than he thought he was worth.

Fortunately for Steve, his wife is extremely supportive. She encourages him to take a chance, to go out on his own as a consultant, despite the risks. As Steve reflects on his situation, he describes his dreams and admits that they look pretty dim right now.

In an angry world, we all have to find a safe place. Sometimes it is in a relationship with another—a spouse, a close friend, a family member.

Some of us just check out. We seem to go into something like a trance. We are there, but we are not really there. We function in the world, but detached from ourselves and not willing to deal with the reality and frustrations of what is going on around us. The point is—we all find a way.

FISHING

Anger can be expressed openly in our home. Violence and acting out destructive behavior are not all right.

One Saturday morning my son was watching *Power Rangers* on TV. After the show, he practiced his karate moves, landing several blows on the body of our golden retriever, Oliver. Although Oliver was unfazed, I could not let the behavior go unnoticed.

My son loves to fish and has a Mickey Mouse pole that he cherishes. As punishment for his behavior, I put his fishing pole away for that day. My wife and I thought that we had made our point, and that his inability to fish that evening would surely get his attention.

That evening as I drove into our driveway I noticed our five-year-old son standing by the lake behind our house. When he saw the car, he screamed, "Daddy! Daddy!"

As I walked toward the lake, I noticed my son had a small yellow bucket in one hand and a length of blue nylon cord in the other. I said, "Son, what are the rope and bucket for?" He replied, "Dad, we are going bucket fishing." Well, I thought this would soon get boring. We would try for several minutes, catch nothing and then go to the house for dinner.

I asked him, "Exactly how do you bucket fish?" He said, "Dad, just tie the rope to the bucket and throw it out as far as you can. Give me the rope and when I pull it in, we will catch a fish."

I did a good job of tossing the bucket out into the lake and then sat back to observe. On the first try, my son caught a fish. For the next two weeks every time I suggested that we go fishing, my son would reply, "Sure, Dad, but let's bucket fish."

I guess, looking back at this, there is a lesson here. Things do not always turn out as you've planned. Or maybe, through the eyes of a child, almost any old lemon can be turned into lemonade.

THE STRING

We live in a time when anger or turmoil inside is judged as evidence of something incomplete, something lacking and as something to be done away with. Gurus and dime-store psychologists try to sell us a bill of goods called "perpetual happiness and fulfillment." This bill of goods presupposes that we must "do" something or correct something if we feel out of sorts, angry or frustrated. The fact that all those emotions are part of what comprises us seems to elude them.

The path is never completely clear. Never. But some of us don't accept that. We want to know what's up ahead and around the next bend. Then if it looks like we're going to feel bad about it, we can nip it in the bud.

I know that not one of the plans I've made to try to prepare myself for the future has ever panned out. None of the dire predictions I've foretold for myself has ever taken place. What *has* happened? I've usually had to revise my plans because most things have turned out far better than I could have imagined.

What I do want to know is what I've been afraid of all these years. What do I run from when it gets too close? What if I kept pulling the string on my fears all the way back to the beginning?

I wonder what I would find at the other end.

GUY'S STORY:
THE BAD NEWS—THE GOOD NEWS

Yesterday I lost it.

My lover was preparing a dinner party for a few people and was in a state of high anxiety. Everything had to be perfect, down to the last detail. I committed the unpardonable sin of walking into the living room with a runny piece of cheese in my hand. I was simply going to put in on the plate with the other cheeses on the coffee table.

I was met with a glare so murderous it stopped me cold. "How could you walk out with a piece of cheese dripping like that? It's probably dripped all over the floor. Where did you grow up, in a pigsty?"

The words don't nearly convey the venom behind them. For an instant, I saw an expression of hatred so fearsome it nearly knocked me over. He looked like he wanted to kill me. It was as though the accumulated frustration of his thirty-five years had suddenly condensed into a single hateful stare.

Whatever it was, it set something off in me as well. I lost it. I don't remember my exact words, but they were something like: "How dare you talk to me like that? Why are you upset over something so stupid? I'm not dripping the goddamn cheese on anything. You know, you treat me like garbage, and right now I hate you!"

Hot tears welled. My words shot out of me. My throat still hurts today from how savagely I yelled at him.

Overreaction? That's an understatement! I couldn't hold back my rage; I couldn't control the explosion. The force of my rage frightened my lover badly; he cowered in front of me. The way I screamed was just as abusive as if I'd hit him as hard as I could. Something kept me from hitting him, thank God. I did throw the cheese on the table, but I didn't throw it, or anything else, at him.

I had truly turned into somebody else—somebody even I didn't fully know. A rage inside, that I had done almost everything to repress throughout my life, exploded. And in my lover's own hateful words and glare at me, I recognized the same violence and anger in him. We had crashed into something in one another that did not even seem human. We saw murder in each other's eyes and souls. It was horribly unnerving. For a moment, we felt as though our worlds were coming undone.

But he and I had enough of a grip on reality to know almost instantly after this explosion that we had tapped, however inadvertently, something a lot more powerful than anger at the prospect of a little cheese dripping on the rug. Through this apparently inconsequential and minuscule moment, two lifetimes of backed-up rage seemed to erupt volcanically, simultaneously, and embarrassingly as well. How could something so obviously silly release such powerful and destructive rage? What was wrong with us?

Anger held to be justifiable, such as that against rape, child abuse, prejudice, against any sort of patently unjust or willful malicious treatment by one human being of another; against an "act of God," such as a plane crash or hurricane; or against an illness, such as cancer, AIDS or Alzheimer's disease is relatively easy to acknowledge. In these cases, there clearly seems a "right" side and "wrong" side. The villain is easy to identify. It's the bigot, the sexual abuser or the raging disease over which there seems to be no control.

But anger that seems to come from *nowhere* (or worse yet, from within us), anger that often seems to come from such minor annoyances as who doesn't put the cap back on the toothpaste tube, can leave us fearful and feeling that there is something violent and uncontrollable at the center of us. This anger that rages at the trivialities in our lives seems to have only one intent: to hurt anyone in its path—including the people we love.

It's not surprising that we'd be terrified of this rage—who wouldn't be? However, as I reflect on the difficulty I've had throughout my life expressing my own rage, I realize it's not only anger that has terrified me; it's conflict of any kind. Any negative ripple in my consciousness, any discomfort, any confusion or frustration has always signaled trouble—an indicator that something was sick, wrong or bad in the center of me, something I instantly needed to "fix."

We live in a culture that encourages this urge to fix anything that seems inconsistent or irrational or destructive. It is, I think, self-evident that most Americans do not see conflict as anything but a deviation from what's "normal." We leap to label as "dysfunctional" uncomfortable emotions, feelings that seem to have no rational source and those with effects that are seemingly toxic. We search for boogeymen to blame and find many: inadequate parents, terrible teachers, abusive partners, bad genes. Most self-help pundits instantly regard any evidence of rage as something to be fixed. The explosion of, and dependence upon, antidepressive medication is very telling. Prozac, Zoloft, Xanax and their derivatives have become the new gods in our psychic universes. With religious fervor we turn to them to rid ourselves of evidence of any uncontrollable darkness, any perverse negative impulses that seem to lurk within us. Our terror of our inner potential to explode, to rage and to hurt can seem beyond our ability to handle. Some of us flee to alcohol, drugs, and/or sex to defuse this toxic anger. Some of us flee to doctors or religion, or some narrow philosophical or political view which we believe can answer everything and provide instant comfort to any blip of unease in us. We regard conflict as intolerable. We do not understand it. We don't like it. We will do anything to rid ourselves of its effects, to kill it at its source.

These attempts to flee our own conflicts, by whatever means, are ultimately doomed. Sooner or later we discover we're attempting to escape some of the most fundamental urges that propel us. Ultimately, the truth is that each of us is angry just by the fact that we exist physically in the world. It's not Mommy's and Daddy's or America's fault. Conflict, frustration and anger are all part of the bargain of being alive—of existing. Our aggressive urges turn out to be as ineradicable as our urges to breathe, sleep, eat or reproduce.

Freud first codified this bad news when he acknowledged that there is a powerful death instinct in each of us, a movement toward entropy and destruction, which will always be at war with the equally fierce libidinal, or life, instinct, the urge to connect, to build, to create—all the urges we like. Freud suggested that anxiety is our normal, inescapable and eternal state of being, although of course it varies in degree from moment to moment and from person to person.

But how could anxiety at the eternal life-and-death tug-of-war inside us not be our normal state? It's how we're made. We have no choice but to accommodate this internal war; we cannot escape its realities or its effects. We cannot drug it out of ourselves, either through some well-meant prescription of Prozac or a junkie's syringe full of heroin. The inescapable human dilemma is not only that destructive, aggressive and angry urges exist in every one of us, but that each will find expression whether we want it to or not. A volcano will erupt—exploding or imploding—but lava must flow. We may hate our own inevitable angry reactions and explosions, but our psyches have no choice but to accommodate them. The lava may cause a deep-rumbling earthquake or a messy eruption, but it's going to cause something we or the people around us aren't going to like.

There's an even more exasperating kicker: The aggressive urges in us—the urges from which anger and rage proceed so terrifyingly—are things that we depend upon to survive. The death instinct almost always meshes with the life instinct, and like yin and yang, neither one can exist without the other. So the news that we're stuck with our anger isn't all bad. Our psyches continually make ingenious use of the dark and light forces within us to create, not destroy. The fierceness of our inescapable anger can and does fuel some of our richest awakenings and most life-affirming and constructive accomplishments. The same force that underlay my anger and rage at my lover also fueled my ability to get through the day, accomplish anything, sit at this computer screen and think up and type out these words. Anger and aggression can both destroy and create. The roots of the anger I hated in myself were as essential to me as the air I breathe; I need it to live, and I need it to create.

Reflecting on the attack and counterattack over the dripping cheese and my thoughts since then, I realize I may not need to be so afraid of anger. I'm curious about its explosive energy. I want to look at it a bit more carefully, not just cut and run from it. I think anger has much more to teach me. For example—how does it mesh and interact with more obviously constructive urges? What role does this force play in my life? When it erupts as it did between my lover and me, what was it trying to tell each of us? Was there more to our outbursts than the raging and screaming we did at each other? What were we screaming for?

Perhaps anger doesn't have to be so horrifying. Perhaps it's not sickness. Perhaps it's one very effective way the unconscious tries to flag our conscious mind down, letting us know something needs attention—and needs it bad. Now, when I think of what my lover yelled at me, I wonder what condensed rage was buried in his fury and his words. When we calmed down a bit, he filled me in: "I'm always a nutcase whenever anyone comes over. I turn into my mother. If you think *Mommy Dearest* was bad, you should have seen what happened at our home when we didn't get a spot off a glass or knocked an ashtray on the floor.

"But it's also got a lot to do with me. I'm a perfectionist about visual stuff. I enjoy getting things so that they look exactly like the picture of them I have in my head. It feels like you're attacking when you mess things up, even if it's only accidental. So I went off the deep end."

I thought of what might be condensed in my own murderous scream back at him. I tried to explain to him as I tried to explain to myself: "It was the look of hate in your eyes. It was as though, for that moment, you really didn't love me. I felt attacked, vulnerable and very, very unsafe. It brought up a lot of things from my past—the feeling that I had to perform perfectly to get attention, much less love. Your look and your tone told me far more than that I had disappointed you—it told me I'd disgusted you."

It was amazing how much more was going on in our outbursts than each of us knew. Not that we're only angry now
because of various screw-ups in our childhood (no worse, after
all, than the childhood of any other average human being). As
I've suggested, frustration and anger are central to what fuels us.
They are inevitable reactions. The goal isn't to understand or
empathize our way out of expressing rage again (fat chance of
that). But when the urge to rage hits, it might, for just an instant,
signal us that something very deeply rooted is trying to be seen
and heard. We may still yell our heads off—in fact, we undoubt-
edly will yell our heads off again. But there might be a tiny bit
more "air" around that yell, the knowledge that something more
important is going on than whatever triggered the outburst.

Anger, like any highly charged and deeply rooted emotional
reaction, has embedded in it some of the most fascinating and
important information about ourselves that we can possibly discover. How it feels in the moment may be terrifying or deeply
embarrassing. Our first, very normal, reaction may be to flee
after we've vented our anger. But that doesn't mean it's sick or
something to be ignored or stamped out. It's a powerful, com-
plex message from the unconscious—so urgent that it will not
tolerate being ignored. It's the steam hiss of a psychic furnace
that keeps us alive, protects us and attempts to guide us.

It is dangerous, no doubt about it. We may need to cultivate
a great deal of self-control in how we deal with it, making sure
the outburst vents itself in words, not fists or frying pans. We
need to give the anger space to be heard and listened to, not just
feared or stamped out with drugs, self-hate or limp bromides
about how "love conquers all."

So, I'll remember this the next time my lover is having a dinner party. But if I should spill something on the tablecloth or the

carpet and he lets me have it . . . well, I'll try to pay attention to what he's saying and what's beneath it.

After, of course, I've finished telling him off.

STEVE'S STORY

When you start your career, you start with lots of dreams. You work hard, save a little money, invest a bit for the future, and imagine a steady rise either up the ladder or on to new and higher paying challenges elsewhere. It seems like you've got all the time in the world.

But we all know that's an illusion. One day you're out of college, in your first job, and have started a home and a family. The next day, it seems, you're in your mid-forties; you're still doing fairly well, but the walls seem to be closing in a little faster. No reason to panic yet, though.

That's what I thought—no reason to panic. After all, I was doing well, had just gotten a raise and a promotion and a little more responsibility. But there was something nagging at me at work. I didn't know at first whether I was just being paranoid or not. Sooner than I expected, however, I found out.

I had survived several "downsizings." That's what they call layoffs these days. The two I'd been through had been completely unexpected. Everyone who was let go had been caught totally off guard. They walked in one Monday morning, and it was over. No parties, no pats on the back, just "good-bye."

After the second downsizing, I exploded at a department meeting. You know, one of those get-togethers where they call the human resources department in to tell you white is black, day is night and up is down. If you've ever been in one of these things, you know what I'm talking about.

The meeting wasn't ugly at first, but I made sure it got ugly before too long. Two of my closest colleagues had been let go, people who'd worked hard and been supportive for years. Sarah was a year short of retirement, and all her benefits were nearly wiped out. She got a year's pay and a boot out the door. She was sixty years old. Where the hell was she going to find another job at her age? And Carl—fifty-five years old with a family and a couple of kids about to go to college. Same deal with him as well.

By the end of the meeting, I was screaming at the human resources people. "Of course you can be so smug about it!" I yelled. "It's not your ass that's being tossed out into the street. You must feel pretty good. With all the people we're dumping these days, it looks like you guys have got some job security. And why the hell can't you just be honest about it? The worst thing of all is that you stand up there and pretend you care when you don't. You're not even faking it very well, in fact."

I didn't hear their reply because by that time I'd gotten up and left the meeting.

Everything was pretty quiet for the next three or four months. No more layoffs—didn't even hear anything through the grapevine. But inside I was still angry. You see, business was better than ever when the downsizings came. That's why things came as such a shock. Seems some of the major stockholders were grumbling about the profits being down and about the stock losing some market value. The raw materials we use in our business are nonnegotiable. We can't do without them. What happened, however, is that the company decided to save money, not by boosting sales, but by cutting jobs that saved the company over 15 percent in salaries—the biggest expense. That way we could keep our prices down and still look good. So next time you want to crow to someone about what a deal or great buy you got on something, just remember that somebody probably paid a pretty high price for your comfort.

Like I said, however, everything seemed pretty quiet. Then they hired Grant, a twenty-six-year-old with a brand-new M.B.A. I liked Grant. He worked hard and did his best to learn the business as quickly as he could. Gradually, however, he started taking over some of the responsibility I held. No problem, I was told—we just want him to become familiar with as many aspects of the business as possible. That's when the sense of foreboding began to set in again. And I was right. Within a year I was basically a fixture, a piece of furniture. Grant was even approving the department's expenditures.

Then one Friday afternoon, the bomb finally exploded. I was told I was being terminated and that, after eighteen months on the job, Grant was going to assume the title I had worked twenty-four years to get. Like I said earlier, it was about money. Grant didn't know it yet, but I knew that he was making less than half my salary.

I was handed a year's severance pay. Phil, my boss, couldn't even look me in the eye. He kept his eyes glued to his desk. I don't even know whether he looked up long enough to see me kick over the bookcase as I left his office.

Anyone want to hire a fifty-five-year-old middle manager? I was glad I got the severance since I made a pretty good yearly salary. The pension I'd built up over the years was pretty nice, as well. I just hadn't expected I'd have to start dipping into it more than ten years before retirement age. I also had the expenses to go with the salary, a daughter who'd be ready for college in a year and another daughter who'd be college-age in three years.

The first year was difficult. We were able to manage financially. But there came that day when I had to liquidate the pension fund. Just to let you know—the government takes 20 percent of that right off the top. I had lots of job interviews that year, but when it got to crunch time, no one wanted to hire someone in his mid-fifties who would only be around for, at the most, ten years. Pretty funny, isn't it—you get let go after twenty-four years then can't get hired because you won't be around that long. I got offered a couple of similar jobs at about 60 percent less than I had been making; Then I got offered one at least 50 percent less; I had to take it.

But it was well over two years after my layoff that I got that job. The severance was gone, and with my daughter in school, the pension fund had taken a hit as well. I must admit I haven't been too productive in this new job because I've still got a lot of anger and resentment inside at the way I was let go.

I didn't think I had much of an ego, but I do. It's tough working just as hard, being the oldest guy in the department, having bosses fifteen years younger than I am and making a lot less money than they are. I really haven't dealt with things all that well.

And it's hurt things at home. My wife said she wanted me to go to counseling because my anger and sullen attitude were getting hard for her to deal with day in and day out. Even though our new insurance wouldn't cover it and it would just be another out-of-pocket expense, I decided to get help, but it took a few months of prodding and shoving to get me there. And it's helped somewhat, though I think it will still be some time before I can let go of all of this.

I don't intend for this to be a sob story. There are lots of people out there who've been left in far deeper trenches than I have; at least I had some financial support to fall back on. I know of people who had literally nothing when they were told it was over. They lost pensions, everything. I don't apologize for my situation, though. I had a lot of dreams that look pretty dim right now, though I haven't given up hope. We've cut back expenses as far as we can. We've even moved to a smaller home.

I'm pretty good at what I do. Since I got let go, I've taken a few small "troubleshooting" consulting jobs that have come along. I kind of liked the work—I think I'd do well at it. I've thought of soliciting some more but frankly have been scared. If I decided to do it full-time, it would mean even more financial insecurity.

My wife, however, sees it a little differently. She's supportive of my getting out and "doing it"—she's been living with this funk I've been in for a long time. She's told me that I'd be good at it and that if she had to choose between the financial insecurity and me sitting around being miserable, she'd take the first.

It's a big step. I just don't know whether I'll take it.

TAKE YOUR TECHNOLOGY AND . . .

I got my first "real" job at a small book-publishing house back in 1978. As an assistant editor, I would dutifully (most of the time) copyedit the manuscripts that came in. Once I finished my work, I would walk the manuscript down a flight of stairs to the office of our production manager, Hattie. She would rage for a few minutes about the manuscript being a couple of hours late, then give me a pained smile that said, "I'm trying to be tough here, but it's not working." Then I'd head back upstairs to my office to start on another manuscript.

In a couple of weeks, the manuscript I turned in would be sent to me in two sets of typeset galleys. I'd send one to the author, correct the other, iron out the differences with the author and then turn the galleys back in. After that I would proof pages and bluelines, and then await the printed book. There would be some glitches in the process from time to time, but for the most part things went pretty smoothly. I spent most of my time going back and forth with authors, which is what book editors should spend their time doing.

But not anymore. Today, as a writer and freelance editor, I don't send publishers manuscripts. I send computer disks. They get the raw copy of the edited manuscript as well, but that's not nearly as imperative as that all-important disk.

As a freelance editor, publishers send me an original manuscript, but also the all-important disk. Let me play out a recent scenario for you—a scenario that gets the anger and frustration level skyrocketing. Ready?

I get the disk and pop it into my computer (a nice Macintosh, by the way—the only way I will give up my Mac is when they pry it from my cold, dead fingers). The following boxed message then appears on my screen: "The disk is unreadable by this Macintosh. Do you want to initialize it for the Macintosh?"

I click "Yes."

"This will erase all the information on this disk."

I press "Cancel." Then I call the publisher.

"Hello."

"Hello. Yes, that manuscript disk you sent me won't open on my machine. I have a Mac."

"We loaded the manuscript on a PC."

"Sorry, I don't own one of those mind-numbing leviathans. What do we do now?"

"We have a couple of Macs here. We'll put it on one of those and express the disk to you."

"Sounds good."

Meanwhile, I'm editing the raw manuscript. I'm eventually going to have to transfer all my written changes onto their disk—another exciting experience. I recommend it to anyone suffering from insomnia.

The new disk arrives. The translator software I've got installed picks up some of their word processing system (Rich Text Format) but doesn't pick it all up. I take a look at what I've got. Some of it's okay, but most of it looks like an obscure Sudanese dialect. I try to translate one more chapter. My machine freezes. When I restart it, I find my system folder has been rearranged; it's shut off some of the systems and thrown several other items out of the system folder and onto the desktop. It takes me more than four hours to get everything back in place again.

Later on I go to see a friend who has a Mac and knows more about this stuff than I do. He bravely loads the disk into his machine. His Mac freezes a few times, and he has to do a lot of starting and restarting. Ultimately, he ends up with the same results I got.

"What word-processing format is it in?" he asks.

"Rich Text Format."

"That's funny; it should work. Maybe they've got a more updated version of that format now."

"Sure looks like it."

I go home and call the publisher. Overnight comes another disk, another seventeen dollars spent.

Load it up—same result. I start throwing things around my office, swearing and hitting the machine a few times, thinking that will do the trick. My wife heads out to the mall for some peace and quiet.

Next day. In the mail I receive an upgrade for my translator program. I install the program, try the disk again—and it works! Never mind that it took an act of God and the U.S. mail to do it. It works. I've finished editing the hard copy by this time, so I start plugging in the changes. I run across a page or two of something that looks like ancient Greek, but nothing much. Hell, by now I'm so grateful I don't even care.

I finish the work, retranslate the manuscript from my word-processing program to the publisher's and send it down. Two weeks later I get a call telling me that there are a number of portions that look like ancient Sudanese. So I translate it again, send it down and get the same call. The long-suffering editor says, "Just send it down in a straight text format. If that doesn't work, we'll just have to retype the entire manuscript with your changes." He pauses, then says what I'd been thinking: "You know, we probably could have been done with this already if we'd just retyped it when you sent it in."

Exactly.

I enjoy good literature. I imagine at times what it would have been like if some well-known author from the past had to go through this process. I can hear it now.

"Mr. Faulkner?"

"Yes?"

"We received your manuscript a couple of days ago. I'm calling from the word-processing department."

"Yes?"

"Well, sir, I've been told to contact you about a problem. In our manuscript submission guidelines, we require that the author submit a disk in MS DOS format for PCs. I'm afraid this looks like it was done on a manual typewriter."

"It was. That's the way I work best."

"Well, it may be, sir, but our manuscript guidelines are very specific about what we require."

"Look, I've already published a couple of books with you. This is nonsense."

"Actually, sir, it really helps us streamline manuscript functions."

"Like I said, I've already published a couple of books with you. What the hell do you think you're doing?"

"I'm sorry, sir, but we do require that the manuscript be submitted in MS DOS format before we can begin working on it. And I've also pulled up our sales-tracking charts—it seems your first two books . . ."

"This is ridiculous. If you won't work on it, then I'll find a publisher who will."

"They'll probably want the same format, too, Mr. Faulkner."

"Hell with that! I'll take my chances."

"I was told that might be your response. Let me see. . . . I've just pulled up our manuscript submission log. Yours is number 834-009-418-A, title, *The Sound and Fury.* Do you want me to delete it?"

"Hell yes! And send me that manuscript back. It's the only copy I've got."

"Certainly, sir. Maybe you'd be better off going with another publisher. I took the liberty of reading through the manuscript a little, and I must admit that a lot of it was pretty hard to understand. It just wouldn't fit our target market."

VERBAL ABUSE

Here's the situation: You've let your ego and your anger get the best of you. You're in a group of people, and suddenly the conversation turns to a discussion of someone you don't like. This individual committed an injustice (either perceived or real) against you in the past. Of course, if you've acted as I have before, you've never really talked with or confronted the person. You've just stewed in your own anger juices and worked up a really good case of high blood pressure.

The discussion gets livelier. People begin dumping their garbage all over this poor, underrepresented soul. You figure, *"What the hell?"* and jump in feetfirst with your own litany of the person's evils and shortcomings.

And it's fun, isn't it? The longer you keep talking, the more of a jerk this person becomes and—surprise, surprise—the better you feel. When the conversation is over, you feel almost cleansed—purged. Boy, it was great to get all that out of your system. You created a monster and killed it, all in a matter of minutes. You really got your anger out.

Cut to a time later that evening. You were at the mall till closing time. You sit in your car, turn the key and . . . nothing.

Fuming, you despair of getting help this late at night.

You're livid, pounding the steering wheel, when a voice suddenly interrupts. "Need a jump?" says the friendly face. You guessed it—the guy you'd been trashing that afternoon bails you out of a jam and cheerily waves good-bye. The only problem remaining now is what you are going to do with all that guilt.

This example may be a little far-fetched, but just a little. In one form or another, this has happened to me a number of times, and usually within such a short period of time that the ring of my insults hasn't yet died down. The individual I've denounced will make a kind remark to me or help me out with a problem I've been having. In one instance I found out the person had said something complimentary about me—actually considered me a friend.

These events are very spiritual. God's deliberately planned a few kicks in the pants to wake me up. I hope I've learned something along the way, because the next kick may not involve kindness.

I've picked up several lessons as a result of these experiences. First, the injustice I imagined was usually just that—imagined. The person had no idea he or she was doing something to upset me.

Second, anger at imaginary wrongs wastes a lot of energy—energy that could be better spent walking in the opposite direction of gossip.

Finally, people deserve the respect of direct contact, not a cheap shot from their blind side. When I feel someone has hurt or wronged me, I have a responsibility to talk with that person face-to-face and check things out—honestly.

And who knows? I might even gain a friend.

On the Road
to Somewhere

INTRODUCTION

Life is random and often capricious. Pain and the resulting anger abound. We are just starting to understand the language of this anger and its many expressions.

The people featured in this chapter feel that their lives are out of control. They experience what can be called "cognitive dissonance" and are vulnerable to disorganization. Instead of assuming their own responsibility to maintain their sense of self, these individuals experience an increased need to allow others to do it for them. Alan strives to get support from a supervisor, while Clay looks to the dean of his graduate school for validation. As you read these stories, you will begin to understand the increased feelings of failure that come as people realize their own limitations. This realization increases their resentment and personal pain as they spiral more and more out of control. The resulting sense of injustice leads to a resentful and bitter demeanor.

The people featured in this chapter play out their own sense of shame and envy as they try to control an uncontrollable world. They engage in activities that strive to give them an illusion of control. In fact, life defies control, but somehow we always seem to be on the road to that place where we can really be in charge. But this illusion of control is fleeting. Just when you think you have it, it slips away. Behind the face that states, "I'm fine" lies the darkness. The opening poem, "Topsy-Turvy," probably sums it up best. In this poem the reader will hear the words "Why I feel impotent and afraid."

The poem goes on:

> But then I'm up in the morning, back at it and smiling;
> The thieves winning the race and the honest folks
> got the creditors banging at their door.

It perplexes us that most people cannot accept the randomness of the world. Human history documents people's constant striving to control their surroundings. Having something in our control—grasping it—is at best a momentary phenomenon.

Life is a search for interpersonal and personal meaning within a context of chaos. No matter how rich or how poor, we all need to connect with ourselves and with others. We all want to feel wanted, loved and cared about. In Mother Teresa's Nobel Prize acceptance speech, she stated, "I choose the poverty of our poor people. But I am grateful to receive it (the Nobel) in the name of the hungry, the naked, the homeless, the crippled, of the blind, of the leper, of all those people who feel unwanted, unloved, uncared for throughout society, people that have become a burden to this society and are shunned by everyone." I have often wondered why so many of us thought she was talking directly to us. Even those with nice cars, nice families and great jobs felt the emotional impact of her statement. We all desire to feel wanted, to feel loved and to feel cared for. Even when the trappings of success are all around us, we may feel a sense of emptiness—a spiritual void that seems to consume us, our families and communities. Mother Teresa, a tiny octogenarian, was a larger-than-life symbol of hope and kindness in this incredibly confusing, materialistic and angry world. She was a beacon for those who feel out of control of their lives, those of us who just want someone to care. When someone cares, we don't have to shoulder our burdens alone.

The baby boom generation started to come of age in the 1960s. As Robin Williams said, "If you remember the sixties, you weren't a part of it." The sixties seemed to have precipitated a narcissistic (sometimes drug-induced) wave that is still carrying us toward the next millennium. The sixties was all about "doing your own thing." It was a time of "me first." It was the beginning of a culture of narcissism that hit its peak in the 1980s. The slogan for the era was: "He who dies with the most toys wins." Materialism was in full bloom; it was more important to possess than to be cared for. It was more important to have a nice car, a nice home, alphabet soup behind your name and be a member of the right country club than it was to contribute to society and give something back. As a matter of fact, when was the last time someone asked you about your values? What do you believe in as an American? How good a parent are you? What church do you go to? How much do you give back to your community? In a materialistic world we can never connect because regardless of whether you have two or two million dollars, you know it's not enough. There's always that drive that pushes us to get more. Our internal world depends on our external world; what we have materially defines who we are. The symptoms of a materially based world are anger, depression and anxiety. Shame and envy are products of the belief that the messages we get from the world about our worth are valid. We internalize those values and are always comparing ourselves to others. Am I better than that other person? Do I have more than they do? We worry when we don't.

We feel out of control: *If only I had that new car, I would feel all right. If I get that promotion, life will be beautiful.* The disease of the "if only's" compromises our ability to understand ourselves and discover what we are really like on the inside. It is only by understanding our essence and accepting our vulnerabilities that we can be open to connection to others and to a higher power. Without this understanding, we feel slighted by the world and slightly paranoid that the world is out to get us.

In a spiritually based world, we are a miracle simply because we're here. A spiritual world involves connection. Today many will try to connect through drugs, sex and other addictions. They will try to connect with what might be described as "the New Age spiritual bypass." They will try any new solution that comes down the pike, anything that promises to make them feel better. These solutions rarely work, however, because they come from the outside. Real spiritual connection is pulling into your driveway and having your seven-year-old son run around the house as fast as his legs can carry him, screaming, "Daddy, Daddy!" and jumping into your arms. Spiritual moments occur constantly. They are easy to identify if one is not consumed by external conditions. In the feature stories of this chapter, both persons experience connectedness, Clay via the caring statements of the dean, and Alan as he takes the time to absorb the blessings of a beautiful spring day.

A lack of spiritual connectedness breeds envy. Envy can lead us into negative and self-destructive behavior. We become angry when we don't have something we feel we desperately need to make us okay. We feel bad when we see other people enjoying what they have—especially if it's a loving relationship. We even, at times, wish the worst for these people. We hope that these people face some setback so they can feel bad, too. People who are overweight may be envious of those who are thin. We envy a friend who owns a beach home. Again, cases of the "if only's." "If only I had these things, my life would be okay." "If only someone would listen." "If only someone would see it my way." These moments in our existence uproot our entire life. It only takes a moment of a real or perceived slight to undermine years of good work. Clay's story is a textbook example of this.

One thing is for sure. Life is not like a television sitcom. There are few, if any, Ward and June Cleavers out there. Ward could handle all the problems on the job, come home and handle all the problems in the house. He could do this in less than thirty minutes and still have time to chuck a little ball with the Beav' in the backyard. A little unrealistic, don't you think? And do you remember that Eddie Haskell? He was a character, wasn't he? Life is not like *Ozzie and Harriet*. If anything, it most closely approximates *The Honeymooners* with Ralph and Alice Kramden.

The story "The Neighborhood Bully" which follows creates a more realistic sense of life. It is a story from the child's perspective, a story of always being one down to the big kid in the neighborhood—never being fast enough, big enough or tough enough to take him on and win. But that one moment when the neighborhood bully is beaten at his own game is enough to inspire us, maybe even for a lifetime. This story teaches us to appreciate the times when we win. This is important because little losses and setbacks are a part of daily life. For example, that loan that looks so easy until you read the fine print or the "quick and easy" instructions that tell you how to put together that Christmas gift that, three hours later and two parts short, looks nothing like the picture on the box. These are examples of life's frustrations, which is the basic theme of this chapter. It is important to stop and reflect, and to focus on the wins instead of being consumed by small setbacks and losses. Appreciate the spiritual moments. Don't agonize over the smaller matters outside of your control. In 1995, Princess Diana said, "The British people need someone in public life to give them affection, to make them important, to support them, to give them light." This is a sad and depressing statement. For in order to be fulfilled, we must search and find the resources within ourselves. Others can assist, but none can give us inner peace.

Unfortunately, life is not fair, but we seem to expect and believe that it should be. Earlier we talked about a sense of vulnerability to disorganization. The result is a sense of injustice or of being cheated. Sometimes this leads to rather asocial thinking. For example, we start to believe that rules don't apply because we've been cheated and that somehow we're entitled to take vengeance on someone to somehow even the score. The story "Road Rage" is about such a situation in America today. The automobile is the great equalizer. It is the equivalent of the six-gun of the old West. No matter whether you're five feet tall and one hundred twenty pounds or six feet tall and two hundred seventy-five pounds, inside of a large metal vehicle, we are equal. All of the bottled up aggression resulting from life's inequities comes out when we're driving.

In an ambiguous world where nothing is either all right or all wrong, we experience anxiety. This anxiety leads to tension and anger. We allow this anger to dissipate by screaming and yelling at other drivers. We get behind someone who's going the speed limit or slightly below and scream at the person. We sometimes blow our horn or say, "Check their pulse—that person must be dead up there."

In the world we live in there is a strong urge to retaliate. We can't always tell our boss to go to hell. We can't always say what we really feel to politicians, police officers or others in the legal systems. We can't even always be honest with our spouses and friends. Imagine this scenario. It's 5:00 P.M., and you're getting ready to leave work on a Friday afternoon. Your supervisor comes to you and says, "This is urgent. I really need to talk with you about your poor performance. Meet me in the office at nine on Monday morning." What would you really like to say to your supervisor at this time? Probably not a compliment.

Don't wait until Monday morning before you read "It's Never Sweet." Notice your emotional makeup as you read this story. This piece is about revenge. You probably can picture yourself swearing at your boss and telling him exactly what you think. You can think about how sweet it will be just to retaliate. We applaud at the end of a movie when the hero has taken revenge on the antagonist, who lies dead or whose life is now ruined. However, what would separate us from the psychopath if we were to actually carry out such revenge? The answer is that we would feel remorse. We're speaking of one of life's double

binds. If I tell my boss how I really feel, it will cause me a problem, and if I don't tell him how I really feel, it will cause me a
problem. Whether I externalize or internalize my feelings, there
are emotional consequences. No, life is not like the movies. It
is full of ambiguity, anger, depression and rage. Fortunately, we
have the spiritual relationships with our families, friends and
higher power that allow us to have those moments when we
transcend the chaos of everyday life.

"Clay's Story" speaks of this chaos. Here we see a young man
who had spent many years preparing for an important moment
in his life. On the way to his graduate school interview, everything went wrong. He experienced a flat tire. His clothes were
soiled, and his spirit was damaged. He asked himself, *How
could this have happened?* These were all negative changes that
occurred rapidly after he had planned everything so well. As we
all know, the best-made plans often go awry.

In "Clay's Story," you will see how anger can rapidly turn into
self-pity. Our behavior is intimately entwined with our thinking
and our emotions. If we start to think in a negative fashion, we will
also experience a negative emotional state. This state can be anger,
depression or anxiety, which can lead to self-pity. The resulting
behavior is often a setup for failure. A catastrophic sequence of
behavior then unfolds.

Underlying Clay's anger and self-pity is his fear, the fear that
he is out of control. As the story reveals, he has done everything
right. He has used all his skills to keep a sound internal focus
of control. He feels in control of his day as he sets out for his
interview. A flat tire changes all that. A simple, everyday incident causes him to feel fearful and out of control.

Clay is very fortunate. As he walks into the dean's office, he
feels out of control. He feels that situations outside of him will

influence the final outcome of this interview. However, this story teaches one important point: that as human beings we can influence other's lives in a positive way. Luckily for Clay, he found another human being who was caring, compassionate and understanding.

This story reveals an important lesson in life. Always surround yourself with people who are positive. It is important to connect and have support in a world that tends to alienate and that often appreciates the failure of others.

Take "Alan's Story," which recounts the loss of a job and career after seventeen years of loyal service. And his dismissal wasn't nice—it was cold, calculated and meant to hurt. Alan moves through all the stages of grief, loss, anger, denial, bargaining, depression and acceptance. It is only after this necessary process that he gains hope.

When Alan looks at his world, he sees the dichotomy between the ideal and the real. Ideally, he would be treated with respect and dignity for the work and time he has put into his job. In reality, he feels only anger, confusion and fear at the possible loss of his position. What Alan is experiencing is "cognitive dissonance." The greater the distance between the ideal and the real, the more the dissonance and the more the resulting rage.

Alan feels a need for the job because it represents security. But Alan can feel no security in his position. He grows to understand there are people he can't trust. Throughout the story, Alan expresses his confusion with statements such as "I feel trapped" and "I feel like a slave."

In today's job market very few have security. Many people understand Alan's dilemma and his fear. Many feel out of control of their lives. The questions arise: "How will I support my family if I lose my job?" "Where will I get another job if I lose this one?" For so many, self-concept is tied directly into productivity. Ours is a material world. Americans define themselves by their jobs, their degrees, their houses and their cars. As we stated earlier, a society based upon these standards breeds anger, anxiety and depression. How do you really know whether you have enough? Two is not enough. Two million isn't enough. You always compare yourself to your neighbor. It is only in a spiritual world that we are connected and secure. When we attach our security to a job or to a mortgage, we stay constantly anxious and angry.

In the past, job security was part of the American landscape. It's like Billy Joel's song "Allentown." Allentown is a moderate-sized town in Pennsylvania where most everyone was employed by the steel mills. When you graduated from high school, you got your union card, you went to work, you got married and you had children. Everything was provided for you in Allentown. You had a job for life, medical insurance for the whole family, a retirement plan and few worries about job security. Joel's song is about the closing of the Allentown mills and the death of a dream for thousands of people. The death of that dream is becoming more and more a reality for millions of Americans today. The language, however, has changed. "Layoffs" was too direct a term, so we've tried to soften the blow with words such as "restructuring," "rightsizing" and "downsizing." But though the language may have shifted, the results are still the same. People are losing something of great importance—the ability to control their fate.

In Alan's case, you will learn that he had to discard an old behavior pattern. Despite continued evidence that his company did not have his best interest at heart, he believed it did. He kept striving and working within a system that didn't want him around anymore. This idealism is not bad; it is a quality more cynics should cultivate. But in Alan's case, all it did was fuel his denial and postpone his decision.

Alan's life had lost a lot of its meaning. Over time, however, he was able to flip his perception. Initially, he focused on what he could not control—the future. He was resentful and bitter about what was happening to him on the job. He had the right to feel that way. But with time Alan became more reflective and learned to make the most out of the present. In his story, he says, "I'm still here, and losing this job has not destroyed me."

Alan learns that living in the past and the future is a dead end. He wasn't getting any goodness out of life and felt trapped and depressed. Once he starts to live in the moment, he starts to grow. He gives up the illusions of the dream job. He turns over control to his God and in the end learns to appreciate a beautiful spring day.

Over time, Alan reaches a point of acceptance. Today he's found a new career in a field he enjoys. The way in which he lost his job still hurts, but it doesn't slow him down anymore. He's doing better, but he had to bust up some very ingrained ideas in order to get there.

Finally, the short piece "Henri" brings an important point to the forefront: that we can only understand how *we* feel and do not know how others feel. They come from different experiences, different places and have different expectations. We often project onto others our rage and our hurts. We believe that they must know how we feel and that, obviously, they should respond appropriately. "Henri" is about a father's desire to connect with his son. Unfortunately, the father fails to understand his son's perspective and operates from his own sense of loss—accumulated over many, many years.

When the stress gets too great, we can dissociate. We can

"check out" and create barriers between others and ourselves. When we feel bad, it is hard to be around others who are feeling good, because their goodness and their happiness only make us feel worse. These are the times that we need others the most, the times that we need to connect.

It is interesting and disheartening that during troubled times, the most difficult people to confide in are those who love and care for us—our families and close friends. Many find it easier to confide in a total stranger than a spouse. A relationship is built on trust: that I can trust you not to reject me, even during the tough times. It is as if we were thinking, *Can't you see I'm already beating myself up?* This is our fearful and self-critical self caught between the struggle for intimacy and the risk of further alienation.

Sure, there are random acts of violence. Yes, there is retaliation. However, for the most part, it is only ourselves who can consistently get us into self-defeating behavior. Like the old line from the comic strip "Pogo": "We have met the enemy, and they is us."

Topsy-Turvy

The night.
That's when my anger comes out the hardest;
when the world's asleep and I'm alone to reflect,
to think, to decipher and decode—
To wonder why I'm still where I am in this world
and not further along the road;
why even with the prayer, the hurt goes on,
why even with prayer, the one I love the most
still sits in the corner and cries;
why I feel impotent and afraid—

But then I'm up in the morning, back at it and smiling;
the thieves winning the race and the honest folks
got the creditors banging at their door.

—BILL CHICKERING

THE NEIGHBORHOOD BULLY

You've seen or read the story in lots of movies and books: a bully terrorizes the younger kids in the neighborhood. Time after time, he humiliates them, makes them cry or slaps them around. You wait, praying for the moment when the bully finally gets what's coming to him.

And in the books and movies, the bully does get it; not only that, his humiliation usually takes place in front of everyone in the neighborhood. The revenge is thorough, and boy, is it sweet.

There was a neighborhood bully where I grew up. He was at least three years older than any other kid on the block. We played a lot of street sports in our neighborhood—softball, kick ball, football and soccer. Our neighborhood bully usually had lots of fun tackling, hitting and beating the stuffing out of the much smaller kids.

The bully never, ever lost. Should it look as though he might lose, he would change the rules along the way. If you didn't like his new rule, you could always quit.

We were angry, but we didn't know what to do. Life in our neighborhood was not like the movies. Where we lived, the bully always won, and we always played by his rules.

But one day that all changed.

One afternoon in late summer, all the neighborhood kids, including the bully, were lounging around my backyard. He must have been feeling pretty low that day, because his desire to humiliate was at an all-time high. He had set up a fifty-yard-dash course that ran through the backyard of our neighbor. Our bully was around fifteen, and he was having a great time racing kids ten and eleven years old, beating them by at least five yards, and then laughing just to add insult to injury.

We were all angry and tired. That is, until we found out there was someone else watching the proceedings and getting angrier by the minute—my mother. Mom slammed the porch door shut and tramped angrily across the lawn. She was barefoot. She walked up to our tormentor and challenged him to race her if he was so hot.

He laughed loudly, made a few smart remarks and got in position at the starting line. On your mark . . . get set . . .

It was an incredible race. Mom's face was so red I thought she would have a stroke before she hit the finish line. But hit the finish line she did—about four feet ahead of the startled young man behind her. Naturally, he accused her of cheating by starting early, complained how his leg hurt and then said he had already run a few races, so he was probably too tired.

But no one listened to him this time. In fact, no one listened to him too much at all after that. He still blustered and swaggered about, but no one let it scare them anymore. He went off to college a few years later. I haven't seen or heard of him for over thirty years. But I hope things went well for him.

Life hasn't turned out like the movies since that day in my backyard. But that one time was more than enough.

CLAY'S STORY: THE ROAD TO GRADUATE SCHOOL

I always thought that the road to graduate school was paved with good grades, not necessarily good intentions. Little did I know that on the road to graduate school, I would end up on the side of the road and in a ditch.

I had lived most of my life in the southern part of the United States. I had never suffered through a Chicago winter. The coldest week I ever spent began the first day I arrived in Chicago.

In the South, the temperatures are moderate. Cold to us is a windy, rainy January day with cold rain running down your neck, the temperature at thirty-five degrees. We rarely saw snow. The weather didn't threaten your life.

I possessed no heavy coat or boots or pair of gloves. I had never lived in a place where the cold could kill you.

You might wonder why I moved from such a nice climate to a place where the winds come off the lake, creating chill factors in the negative twenties, thirties and lower. The fact of the matter is I'd applied for graduate school to a prestigious program in psychology. I'd moved to Chicago after being accepted. I was to attend a formal interview with the dean of the school and one of the professors as a part of my entrance requirements. It was to be an oral evaluation of my potential and interest.

On that particular day in February, I dressed in my best clothes and shoes. In my hand I had a map that showed me how to get to the school. I must tell you that the John F. Kennedy and the Dan Ryan Expressways were intimidating. Most of my life had been spent on two-lane back roads winding through quiet countryside.

On Interstate 294 as I was traveling south, one of my back tires went flat. I pulled over to the side of the road to change to the spare. Without gloves or a hat and dressed only in my best suit, I prepared to brave a chill factor of minus twenty-five degrees. As I got the jack out of the trunk and positioned it at the back end of the car, there were many cars and trucks that passed by me. And on the road, snow had now turned into black, gritty slush. My hands were amazingly cold, raw and bleeding in several places. I was adept neither at using the jack nor at dealing with the numbness of the chilling cold. Finally, I completed the job and I got back into the car.

As I sat in the car with my hands in front of the heating vent, I was so angry and tense that I considered turning around and going back to my apartment. I was cursing my fate and saying to myself, *I had everything together, and now what will they think of me? Maybe I should just cancel this appointment and reschedule for another time. Maybe this is just an omen. Maybe I should go back to the South, where things are more comfortable.*

I looked down at my clothes. They were a mess. My nice white shirt was splattered with grime. My shoes were caked with ice. I noticed a grease spot on the front of my coat and another one just over my left eye.

How could this have happened? I had everything so well planned out. I had allowed ample time. I'd put a soothing jazz tape into the cassette deck of the car. I'd worked hard to use all the skills I'd learned in undergraduate psychology to keep my nerves in check. But I was a mess. My nerves were jangled. I was angry at the world. I fully expected that the dean of the school would see me as a candidate for a psychiatric ward, not for a graduate program.

As I arrived at the university, my angry mood had been replaced with one of self-pity. As I walked toward the entryway, I said to myself, *Why has this happened to me? What did I do to deserve this?* I thought they would never accept me.

With trepidation, I entered the waiting area of the dean's office. By the look on the receptionist's face, I knew that she was trying to figure out whether to call security or let the dean know that I had arrived.

As I was summoned into the dean's office, I was already apologizing. As I came through his door, a strong desire to give an explanation led me to tell the story of the last hour. I fully expected the dean to respond in a negative fashion. However, the dean said to me, "I'm more interested in how you look on the inside than how you look on the outside."

I learned a lot from that interview. I learned that I'd not been fair to myself. My negative self-talk had made me feel not only angry, but unworthy. In the course of one hour, I'd totally undermined the good grades, hard work and confidence I'd achieved in the preparation for this important moment of my life. I also learned that projecting your own feelings and thoughts onto someone else is nothing but a hallucination. I'd set up a scenario designed to lead to disaster. Instead, what I had found in another human being was caring, compassion and understanding. I know that the world is not always this way, but I know that there are plenty of compassionate people out there.

From all of this, I learned that the way you think can influence your emotions. In subsequent situations where I have experienced failure, betrayal or anger, I have tried to remember calming statements that seem to help. I say to myself, *Do the best that you can.* Sometimes the Serenity Prayer helps:

> God grant me the serenity
> to accept the things I cannot change,
> the courage to change the things I can,
> and the wisdom to know the difference.

I sometimes think of the words that were shared with me by a friend who is a Buddhist. One day he saw me distraught over some incident that ten days or ten years from then would have little impact on who and what I would turn out to be. This friend said that the dream that I was having then was just like the one I had the night before. Sometimes this helps me to step away from the moment and to appreciate my true position in the world.

I also think it's true that to really experience good times, you have to have some appreciation of the bad times. This day in my life started out as a bad time, but it was from that polar-opposite place that I was able to appreciate the kind words of the dean. From this appreciation I was able to gain knowledge.

By the way, I did get accepted.

ROAD RAGE

Tell me, what is it about Americans and their cars, and their trucks, and their vans and their sport utility vehicles? Something happens to us when we get inside those things. And what happens is not what you see on most television commercials; we don't settle into a plush leather interior and drive down a winding country road with autumn leaves blowing all around us. We don't ease back into a sculpted seat and get ready to experience the comfort of climate-controlled driving while listening to some hip jazz riffs on the CD player.

No. Most of us get ready to go to war. We strap ourselves in tightly and surround ourselves in several tons of steel-plated armor, ready to join thousands of others during the morning or afternoon rush, driving at ridiculous speeds, perilously close together—a bunch of frazzled, stressed-out maniacs. We may not be the boss eight hours a day, but by God we're the boss when we hit the freeway. It seems as though all the aggression we had to keep bottled up during the day comes out when we're driving home. And vice versa: if we had a fight with a spouse or boyfriend or girlfriend the previous evening, or if we got bad news in the mail, everybody gets it in the morning.

I've often wondered why I get so angry when I'm driving and why microscopic problems become huge once I get behind the wheel. Why do I get annoyed if I don't make it through a traffic light? It's only going to be another minute. Why do I get upset if someone gets in front of me? If it's done dangerously, all I need to do is honk my horn. Why do I get enraged when someone in front of me won't go faster? Usually, they're just doing the speed limit anyway—something I might want to consider doing!

Speed-limit signs, by the way, mean nothing. Whether I've been doing five, ten or twenty miles an hour over the limit, inevitably there will be someone right on my tail, informing me that I'm not going fast enough to suit that driver's purposes. Most of the time, they could just get into the next lane and go around me, but evidently, it's important that they send that message. But sometimes I play the game as well. Someone tails me, I get into the next lane to let them go around me, then cut back into the lane I was in and tail them, making comments about their ancestry under my breath. Pretty mature behavior for someone in their mid-forties, don't you think?

Other drivers have called me everything imaginable. And the comments have no demographic limits. I've been dressed out by people between the ages of eighteen and eighty-five. I've uttered a few epithets myself, I'm ashamed to say—mostly of the references-to-ancestry variety and a few others describing various bodily functions. I'm doing better these days, but it's hard to shut up when that blood gets boiling.

What we often tend to overlook when we get angry on the road is that we are at the wheel of a two-ton pound projectile aimed down the road at speeds up to eighty miles an hour and beyond. They're simple modes of transportation that we, in our anger, turn into weapons. If we were to hit someone head-on at the speeds we travel, or flip over, we, and others, would be shredded, maimed and/or killed.

Yelling at someone on the road or making an obscene gesture is not a smart thing to do. Aside from being a country in love with our cars, we are also a country that is the proud owner of nearly 300 million guns; and some of us carry these guns in our car. Some people have used them. Some people have become angry at other drivers, pulled up to them at the next stoplight or driven alongside them on the open road, pulled out a gun and emptied it into them. I'm not talking about isolated incidents; it happens over and over again in America, every day.

Each year, more and more deaths on our highways are attributed to "road rage." We're out there using our vehicles as deadly weapons and slaughtering each other. And why? Because someone cuts us off? Because someone is going too slow for us? Because someone who doesn't know the way is slowing down to look at directional signs? If it weren't so frightening, it would be funny.

Most of us have to get out there and drive. There's simply no avoiding it. And if you drive today, you're going to encounter "road rage" in one form or another. As best you can, leave your ego at home when you get out on the road. If someone cuts you off, don't keep tailing them—let it go. If someone ticks you off, don't follow them for miles, yelling at them and showing them how angry you are—let them move on. And if someone is going too slow for you, don't flash your lights at them over and over, and then squeal around them, making gestures. Wait for an opportunity to pass them, and do it without fanfare. If you're on a road where you can't pass them, ease the throttle down and enjoy the scenery a bit. True, you might be five or ten minutes late for your appointment.

So what?

IT'S NEVER SWEET

That feeling—it's like getting high. The adrenaline's pumping through your system so fast you think you're going to explode, or else explode on someone. You're hurt, and you're angry. Maybe a friend made you angry; maybe you were the victim of a horrible injustice; maybe one of your loved ones was hurt deeply and you feel powerless. You want to strike back.

You can see it in your mind. The picture is so vivid you can almost taste the hatred. You imagine how someone else is going to feel and hurt as you put the screws to that person and tighten, tighten, tighten. You smell the blood, and you want more. Simple humiliation will not be enough.

Perhaps you've been working at a bad job for too long. You imagine what you're going to do and say on your last day. You picture yourself swearing at your boss, telling him or her exactly what you think—in fact, you want to tell all the people you didn't like exactly what you think. Again, you imagine how sweet it will be, how warm and fulfilling, how delicious!

I can't tell you how many times I've imagined how sweet revenge was going to be and just how wonderful it would be to get my anger out by paying someone back for what that individual had done to me. I've had a couple of jobs over the last twenty years that I just couldn't wait to end so I could march righteously into the human-resources office with a script of everyone in management who I thought should be trashed, hurt and fired.

We live in a culture of revenge. Revenge sells. Right now we're in the middle of "sweeps" month in the television industry. Sweeps month usually entails embellishing the programming with more: (1) skin; (2) hard-hitting local reports that you won't see the rest of the year; and (3) violence. And what amazes me is not the violence (hell, I expect gunfire to be the first sound I hear when I turn on the television). What amazes me is that most of the violence is all about "payback." It's about getting even, and about the happiness and relief people experience at the end of a show when the hero's enacted revenge and someone else lies dead, nearly dead or ruined for life. Hugs all around.

For six months the entire country was entranced by the civil trial of O. J. Simpson. We couldn't take our eyes off it. And why? Anger. Revenge. It hits us at our most basic level. Those who believed in his innocence were angry: "Why is he being put on trial again? He was already acquitted." Those who believed he was guilty wanted revenge: "Well, he didn't get his the first time, but this time we'll make him pay."

We thrive on revenge; we thrive on payback—whether it's humiliating someone who hurt us or making a driver miss his exit on the freeway because he cut in front of us a few miles back.

One of the first things I learned when I sobered up more than eight years ago is that holding resentments and needing revenge will send me back to the bottle faster than anything. Recovering alcoholics can survive the death of a loved one, the loss of a job, a financial reversal or serious illness without going back to drinking. What we can rarely survive, however, is holding on to resentments and hanging on to the need for revenge. These things will poison us and frustrate us faster than anything.

I can hear it now: "Well, that's all nice and wonderful and philosophical, but let's get real. That stuff just doesn't work in real life."

I'll admit it—a good part of the time, I feel the same way. But just the other evening, while watching a documentary, I saw a powerful case for letting go and moving on. The footage only lasted half a minute, but the movement of the two men involved spoke volumes: Pope John Paul II was kneeling in prayer in a prison cell. His arms were clasped on the shoulders of a tearful man shuddering with sobs. Months earlier, that same man pulled a gun on the pope and nearly shot him to death. The pope was telling the man he forgave him, that he harbored no resentment or hatred.

It's hard to stay bitter watching a scene such as that.

If you expect that "an eye for an eye and a tooth for a tooth" is going to solve anything, you're sadly mistaken. If you've put this creed to the test, you've probably already learned some lessons: (1) Not all the time, but sometimes, the bad guys win. Sometimes they win big. (2) All the need for payback will do is keep you angry and frustrated. If you've ever enacted revenge and left the object of your anger either literally or figuratively bleeding, how did it feel?

I've been there and done that, so I can tell you how it felt. Like hell.

ALAN'S STORY

I don't have to tell you that one of the things that can frustrate you and cause more anger than most anything else is your job. Sometimes it seems like all you do is go in and fight the politics every day when you really would rather just be doing your work. I recently had an extremely frustrating experience with a job that I'd held for more than seventeen years with a billion-dollar company. I eventually "resigned," but that was just the conclusion of the frustration. The real story takes place before any of that happened.

Frustration and anger had been my reactions to my position for quite a while. I had almost become used to it, if indeed it is possible to get used to those emotions. Every day it seemed as though there was another battle to fight or another skirmish for someone's dearly held territory. It took me a while to begin to recognize how angry I really was. What I began to do to deal with that anger was to go to violent movies and vicariously try to unload some of it. As it is with any quick fix, it worked for a while, but sooner or later it all started to fall apart again.

But I do remember the turning point in all of this. For years I had been trying to get myself heard; I just wanted someone to listen. I had a very responsible position; the welfare and well-being of a lot of people rested on some of the decisions I made. One day I sat down with a supervisor to talk about what I thought needed to be done. His suggestion was to hold another study group or call a meeting and get some feedback on it. Again, as always, there was no hint that any action would be taken. Whenever a meeting or study group was suggested over the course of my seventeen years at this company, I knew it was simply a euphemism for "We're not going to do anything, but just to make you feel good, we'll try to look as if we were."

At that point, after nearly two decades, I checked out. I had reached my saturation point. I guess you could say that I "emotionally resigned."

Someone was hired shortly thereafter to supervise my position. For a while I managed to get some enthusiasm going again. I thought, *Great, a fresh face. Maybe they'll see what needs to be done here. Maybe I'll be able to talk with them.* I decided to trust this new person.

Then my supervisor dropped the bomb. Just when I thought I was going to hear some good news, he told me that I was going to have to let some people go—not deal with the problems, just get rid of some people.

I was so angry that I could barely talk with my wife that evening. I got rid of some of the anger by writing notes in a journal. It was all I knew how to do then.

I didn't think the new supervisor cared about the people. The next day, I told him that I felt he was just using me to get his dirty work done. One day I got really angry at him and let it all out. All he did then was imply that I was in some way unstable. It was another turning point. I realized at last that I could not fix what was going on at work. I also felt trapped. I didn't know where I could get another job and was afraid of walking into the same kind of situation again.

I prayed to God and asked for guidance and direction. What did I need to do? One thing I felt clear about was that I needed to find out what my part was in all of this. How did I need to change my communication style? What were some other ways in which I needed to change? I read a book on communication skills and determined that I needed to be more constructive and more of a team player. Maybe going with the flow would work better than trying to go upstream all the time.

So I became open to feedback and asked my boss to suggest ways in which I could become more effective on the job. The meeting lasted three hours. I heard everything that anyone had ever said about me—all the innuendoes, everything.

That gave me a lot to think about. Though it made me angry, some of what was said was true. I took all my anger and started walking—for over two hours, in fact. I had just heard a seventeen-year list of all my sins read to me. A lot of it was information that I can understand no one would want to tell me. I also realize now that if I *had* been told, I probably would not have listened.

I started thinking about ways to improve things. My boss and I met again. He told me that he didn't think I was the person for the job. I was furious! "First you tell me we can work on things," I told him. "And now you're telling me just the opposite. I feel completely betrayed."

It seemed that no one was being honest with me. The way I figure it, is that if someone has a real problem with me, they're going to tell me, not talk behind my back. I had had performance appraisals for more than fifteen years, and all of them had been glowing—every one of them. People, it seemed, were not willing to admit they had a problem with me.

One day at work my boss called me in—I figured, to fire me. He told me that I was going to be placed in another position. I remember thinking that if I showed my anger, I would lose the little they were giving me. Instead, all I did was calmly say, "Okay. I can see what you're saying."

I felt like a slave. But through it all, I tried to remember: *I am more than this. These people do not define me.* I tried to remain positive. I arranged another meeting toward the end of the week to find out what the new job would entail. I was told that I would have to move down the hall so my former coworkers would not be upset by having to look at me all the time.

It was a very hard year. In the midst of this, my wife's father died, and we had to go through all the arrangements, travel to the funeral, and then deal with the grief that a death within your close family places upon you.

Every day was hard. I would think things through and let my anger bubble up when I went to places like the grocery store. On the job, I was told that I would not have any input concerning the position. At first, it did not occur to me that these people were trying to get rid of me. Then, one day, a short time after I was moved down the hall, I began to laugh. I thought, *I'm still here, and it has not destroyed me.* Later on, a coworker said that if all this had happened to him, he'd leave.

That was a wake-up call. At first I thought, *Well, I should leave, I guess.* Later on I decided that I needed to leave. I had more than a year's worth of rage built up in me, and it seemed to me that the only way to deal with it was to take action in a positive direction and look for some hope in the future.

I talked with my wife, talked to friends and prayed. That helped me to put things in perspective and let go of more anger. The anger eventually subsided for the most part, although sometimes I'm not really sure where it went. It still flares up from time to time, but I expect it to.

Eventually, a decision was made for me. I was given a severance package. I didn't think it was a fair package for someone who had put in more than seventeen years, but at that point I was too tired to fight anymore. I would just have to do my best to let go of the dishonesty and the way in which the company dealt with me.

It's good to be out of that situation. For a while, after I received the severance package, I was too scared to even look for work. I think my anger could have motivated me to leave earlier, had I let it. I know now that I had held false hopes and expectations in all that happened to me. When I left, I talked to people more and spent more time reading the Bible and praying. Since I couldn't find the hope in myself back then, I looked outside for it.

It's been nearly two years now since that ordeal. I've received some good leads for employment, and I'm working part-time. I am less sure that I will ever get my "dream job." Some days I feel okay and others I don't. I spend time talking with God and work on building my trust in him. I tell myself sometimes that this is not a world gone mad, and I seek reassurance every day. That is where I am right now.

I sit here and look out the window. It's spring and everything is alive and blooming. I'm grateful that all that happened to me occurred in spring instead of winter. And if something like this should ever happen again, I hope I'll have the tools in hand to know how to deal with it.

I recently talked to a friend of mine. She'd been looking forward to a vacation at the beach for a long time. She went, and guess what? It rained all week long. So sometimes, I guess, it's just bad luck and sometimes, it's just the luck of the draw.

It's a comfort to know, however, that behind it all is a power much greater than I can imagine.

YOU CAN KEEP YOUR DAMN ANGER!

See if this might describe an incident or two in your past: It's midnight. A man has a flat tire on a deserted stretch of country road. He's miffed that he'll have to change the tire, but knows it shouldn't slow him down too much. He looks in the trunk and then angrily begins throwing things around. Then he explodes. He's left the jack and the tire iron at home. Now what? The only sign of life he sees in the distance is a small speck of light, and he has no idea how far away that is.

The road is steep and winding. As he walks he mutters: "What if I do find some place? It'll be closed anyway. Suppose I can't find anyone who has a jack? What will I do then?"

A few more miles up the road: "Maybe I'll find someone and they'll get angry that I woke them up. Or suppose I wake them up and they yell at me and tell me to get the hell off their property. Or maybe they'll see me coming and call the cops. Then I'll have to bail myself out of jail. I'll be charged with criminal trespassing and have a police record. Then they'll hear about it at work, and I'll get fired. Then my wife will get angry and tell me what an idiot I am for losing my job. She'll probably take the kids and leave."

He is enraged by now. It's almost two in the morning, and his feet are screaming in pain. He sees a farmhouse, limps slowly to the door and knocks loudly. A tired but friendly man opens it and is about to ask if he needs help. Our friend looks up at him and spits out: "You can just keep your damn jack!" Then he stomps back down the road.

Maybe the circumstances differ, but most of us know a similar story all too well. We write an entire drama before the curtain goes up on the first act. We get the heart pumping, the adrenaline rushing, and slowly move our anger to the tip of our tongue.

And then? And then nothing—less than nothing. Quite the contrary, everything goes beautifully—so beautifully, in fact, that we end up embarrassed and swimming in guilt.

I've been primed and ready for a lot of fights that didn't take place and arguments that never got a chance to start. I've written bitter letters that never needed to be written and blurted out phone messages better left unspoken. I've spent as long as a month preparing for a confrontation that was never to be. Whether I'm anticipating a meeting to ask my boss for some time off, an appointment at the bank for a loan or a potentially loaded conversation with a family member, my imagination of the impending situation has always exceeded reality.

But the silliest way I stir up my anger and my worry is in telephone conversations. If I sense a certain inflection in a person's voice or if someone says good-bye a little too abruptly, I immediately wonder what's wrong. Is that person upset with me? Then I stew until the next call. Rather an unprofitable way to spend my time, don't you think?

On and on it goes—much ado about nothing, time wasted and anger misspent, days and weeks spent squirming over what might happen, building resentments that sap my emotional and spiritual energy. And why do I do it? I don't know, because there's never been a payoff.

Frankly, I don't know whether there's a remedy for this. If there is one, I guess it would be age and experience—we simply get so sick and tired of it all that we stop. Or, who knows, maybe we never get over it. Mark Twain put it best. Toward the end of his life, he wrote, "I am an old man and I've worried about many things—most of which never happened."

HENRI

At times, our home is like a zoo. We have two wild peacocks, five ducks, worm ranches, ant farms, two female kittens named Jefferson and Mickey, plus a golden retriever named Oliver. I forgot to mention the aquariums.

Early in the morning, I go downstairs to take a head count and look out over our lake. One morning, I notice that my son's favorite goldfish, Henri, is floating on his side in the aquarium. Speaking of denial, I quickly go make coffee, hoping that when I return, the condition will have improved.

With Henri still floating in the aquarium, I start to get concerned. How am I going to tell my son Camden about this disaster? Henri is his favorite. Pacing the kitchen, I do a dress rehearsal: "Son, I know you loved Henri, and it is okay to cry. If you want, we can give him a good burial in our pet cemetery down by the lake." This is difficult for me since touchy feelings have often been stuffed or ignored. But here I am, trying to break some old patterns, when my son walks into the room. He has on his pajamas with the feet on them and is wiping the sleep from his eyes. He says to me, "Dad, will you get me some juice?" "Sure, Son," I say, knowing that it is now time to tell him about Henri.

My son is sitting on my lap as I tell him the bad news. "Camden," I say, "Henri died last night." I tell him it's all right to cry, to be angry and sad. I tell him that we could give Henri a proper burial down by the lake in the family pet cemetery if he wants to.

My beautiful child stares at Henri for five, ten, fifteen seconds with a serious expression on his face. Finally, he turns to me and says, "Dad, can we cut him open? I really want to see how those fins work."

I never fail to marvel at how the way we look at things differs so greatly and how easy it is to project our hurt onto another: my son's innocent desire to explore, versus my feelings of loss. We all see it differently, and each one of us is right.

SECTION ONE CLOSE:
MANAGING ANGER ALONG THE WAY

Happiness depends, as nature shows,
less on exterior things than most suppose.

—William Cowper

Many movie buffs will remember *War of the Roses*. This movie features Kathleen Turner and Michael Douglas. It focuses on the deteriorating relationship between a husband and wife, and involves both psychological as well as physical warfare. In one scene, Turner turns to Douglas and says, "I want a divorce." Douglas's reply is, "Why?" To this, Turner responds, "Because when I look at you lately, I just want to smash your face in." As was observed in "Guy's Story," it seems that those closest to us are often able to push our buttons more easily than anyone else. In "Guy's Story" the extent of the hostility didn't match that in *War of the Roses*. However, it demonstrates how pent-up anger and rage stored for decades can emerge at the slightest provocation. It seems to come from nowhere.

Jean-Paul Sartre once said, "Hell is other people." This theme was also demonstrated in "Alan's Story." No matter how hard Alan tried to please or to do the right thing, it seemed that there was always someone else in control and calling the shots. Maybe hell is really being out of control of one's life and not knowing it.

Many people feel out of control of their lives today. There is a great distance for many between their personal reality and what the television and movies dictate as our manifest destiny. Many people are angry. Not just angry; they feel that getting even is justified. As we've seen in the preceding chapters, the automobile is one of the great equalizers. It is a way of releasing our anger at some real or perceived slight at the hands of another. It is amazing how often drivers change lanes to have a car behind speed up, tailgate, and then speed around them while flashing a one-finger salute. While the driver who originally changed lanes wasn't the other driver's problem, the incident provided the opportunity for the other driver to release rage.

A sense of being disconnected contributes to the anger, despair and anxiety that so often end up in the psychologist's and psychiatrist's office. Many feel alone. Many are frustrated. Peggy Noonan, the former Reagan and Bush speechwriter, probably summed it up best when she said, "My generation, faced as it grew with a choice between religious belief or existential despair, chose marijuana. Now we are in our Cabernet stage."

Anger is not just about our relationships to other people as we've observed in "Steve's Story" and "Road Rage." Anger is not just something we direct toward others. It is also something that has an incredibly detrimental effect on us. Anger is bad for the heart. A high level of anger may be a better indicator of the danger of developing heart disease and of the chances that a person with a heart condition will suffer sudden death. In a seven-year study of males over sixty, those who had the highest scores in hostility on an MMPI (a standard personality inventory) had three times the average risk of heart attack and fatal heart disease.

Not only is anger detrimental when it is displayed in the form of hostility, but it is also equally dangerous to suppress it.

A Belgian study reported in *The Harvard Mental Health Letter* found that individuals with mild cardiac infarction histories and with a strong tendency to suppress their feelings were 27 percent more likely to die within ten years after their heart attack. It seems that anger may be more dangerous to the heart than competitiveness or even work addiction. Chronic resentment and anger seem to eat away at our insides, leaving us physically vulnerable.

People make you angry. Anger can make you sick. Angry outbursts continue to get you in trouble with spouses, bosses, teachers and others. What do you do about it?

The treatment of anger is extremely controversial. There are many styles and many techniques. Unfortunately, there has been very little research showing that one technique is more favorable than another. Plus, the fact that anger is multidetermined and not easily approached in any one way complicates the formulation of any step-by-step approach. For example, at a prestigious treatment center, I once observed a male of twenty-five, weighing about 200 pounds, going through a psychodrama experience. He had been admitted to this treatment program for spousal abuse and alcohol addiction. It seems every time he got drunk, the alcohol had a disinhibiting effect, and from that came an angry, sometimes violent, outpouring. He had a history of abuse as a child, which included Mom drinking during pregnancy and neglecting him when he was young. During the psychodrama exercise, this young man was wedged between blocks of Styrofoam, covered with a blanket and told to fight his way out as if he were in his mother's womb. After this experience, he lay on the floor, sweating profusely, with tears in his eyes. He had just gone through an incredible outburst of anger and rage. The whole group sat around him in a circle on the floor and told him how wonderful it was that he got in touch with his anger. It seemed to me that his anger had been getting him in trouble for more than ten years. All I saw that day was someone practicing to get angry and violent again. He was to be discharged the next day to go back home. He had learned no new techniques and had not practiced any new strategies that would help him more effectively manage domestic stress.

Most of the books on anger today take a cognitive-behavioral approach to treatment. For individuals who have an emotional override to their intellect (those who are angry, depressed or anxious), cognitive and behavioral styles of therapy seem to serve as an intellectual and behavioral counterbalance to the emotion. One way of understanding this is the following formula: behavior = emotion + intellect. Most therapies have tried to work on emotions, such as anger, by helping an individual get in touch with the cognitive, or thought, processes that occurred in their mind prior to the acting out. This form of therapy has names such as cognitive therapy or rational emotive therapy. The theory is that if individuals understand and can positively change what they're saying to themselves, they have a way of controlling both emotion and behavior. The theory is that the negative things that we say to ourselves on a preconscious level feed into our emotional and behavioral systems, leading to negative emotional and behavioral outbursts (the emotion of anger and the behavior of aggressive acting out for example). On the other hand, many feel that what you can control is behavior, not thought or emotion. The schools of thought that propose this are behaviorism, reality therapy and others. Central to these schools' philosophy is that if we behave in a correct way, this behavior will influence both the way we think and the way we feel. Both schools of thought are correct. Most often we see cognitive and behavioral theory combined into an approach called cognitive-behavioral therapy.

Consider an example of how thoughts can sometimes spiral out of control and lead to self-defeating behavior. You see your best friend talking with your fiancé as you enter a restaurant for lunch. Your mind starts to surmise that maybe there is something going on between them; although, in fact, it was probably just casual conversation. As your thoughts escalate, you start to wonder whether they have ever been together before. As you progress in your thinking, you start to believe that those thoughts are real. You tend to lose the conscious awareness that the thought is not necessarily reality, but only something that you have projected onto the situation. These thoughts take on a life of their own and create a sense of insecurity. This sense of insecurity drives you to look for little clues that might further substantiate these thoughts you have about your now ex-best friend and your fiancé. As you focus on these details, you start to lose sight of the bigger picture. This also triggers old patterns that help you cope with situations that create insecurity. Part of this pattern may be the development of a justifiable rage or anger. This anger sometimes can create a self-fulfilling prophecy. At lunch that day you get into an argument with your fiancé, over something trivial that has nothing to do with your best friend. This war of words validates your thoughts and makes the initial suspicion seem even more real and vivid. This ultimately becomes a vicious cycle. Thoughts that can emerge from this are: "I really trusted him, and now I don't think that I can." "What a fool I was to love such a person." "What's going to happen if we get married and he cheats on me?" "How humiliating will all of this be?" These thoughts can lead to behaviors such as storming out of the restaurant or giving him his ring back. All of this has come from some offhand observation leading to thoughts that in reality probably had nothing to do with the truth.

In cognitive behavioral styles of treatment for the angry individual, there are two basic approaches. The first approach is that of skills building. Many people who are angry can learn, for example, how to solve a problem. They can learn assertiveness. They can use the group to role-play. A technique such as role reversal might be helpful, allowing them to see another's point of view. Feedback from a friend, a therapist or a treatment group can help people understand how their behaviors can bring out an angry or ill-advised response from another. Skills building teaches individuals how to get their needs met in a way that facilitates cooperation and understanding. Other methods involve participation in community-skills building events such as Outward Bound, ropes courses or wall climbs, where a group has to work together in a spirit of cooperation to achieve its goals.

A second style involves manipulation of rewards or environment. For example, a contingency contract might be put into place. Ben Franklin was a wonderful, positive contingency contractor. He noticed that people didn't necessarily want to come to church but they were all in line for rum. So, as a contingency to get the rum, everyone must first come to church, because rum was passed out right after church. The church was filled to the rafters every Sunday. This is an example of what is called a positive contingency contract. The technique involves someone delaying an immediate response, such as getting angry, in exchange for a longer-term positive reward. Techniques such as "time out" are often used with children and adolescents. If a person is taken out of the situation that is provoking anger, a cooling-off period allows that anger to subside. We might also see this in domestic violence situations where the perpetrator has to leave the home for a period of time.

There are many other techniques, such as thought stopping, counting to ten and using cognitive affirmations to change old patterns that build into anger. Many times anger does involve an old pattern, and anything that interrupts that pattern can make a difference. An example of this is as follows. A boss would, on occasion, have an angry employee who would find him in the hallway and express very emotionally how important it was to talk to the boss right away. The boss would express that he understood how important it was that they chat but that first he really had to go to the bathroom. He would ask the employee to meet him in his office in ten minutes. Well, in ten minutes, that person may be far different. The employee may have displaced that anger with something else, and certainly, changing the pattern will have an impact on the situation. When the employee walks into the office, the boss would always say, "I know how critical and important what you are about to tell me is, so you don't mind if I tape record it, do you?" Again, changing the pattern. Often the employee would look at the boss and say, "You just want to show me how childish I'm being, don't you?" Generally, the boss's response is, "Oh, that's only part of it."

One of the newer approaches that can be used to work with issues involving anger is solution-oriented therapy. Solution-oriented therapy focuses on the outcome the client wants to achieve as opposed to the problems and their causes. The clinician encourages the individual to identify what will be different when the problem is resolved. The question of what will be different when the problem is no longer present is often described as the "miracle question." The clinician then helps the client connect with his past history of successes in dealing with similar situations, help identify exceptions to the problems and evaluate small, but very significant, positive changes. This allows the client to gain confidence in his own competencies and focus directly on positive, useful changes as opposed to historical reasons for the problem.

There are numerous other beneficial strategies including meditation, biofeedback, exercise and nutritional regimens (including the supplements found in health food stores). Body therapies, such as massage, can also be useful. Alone, these strategies seem somewhat incomplete. For example, if your airplane is going to crash, a supplement such as kava kava would be nice to calm your nerves but would not save your life. It might be more helpful to put on a parachute (behavior), remember the procedure used to jump from the plane (thought) and engage the parachute.

One of the most difficult problems in dealing with anger is the fact that you cannot change things you do not believe you can control. You see, anger is always somebody else's fault. When you listen to angry people, they will generally say something like "I was angry because you ignored me at dinner last night" or "I was angry because of something you said to my mother." What this indicates is that anger is generally projected to be somebody else's fault. How do you change that which you do not control?

There are many aspects of anger that get in the way of change. Ray DiGuseppe, professor of psychology at St. Johns University, discusses the aspects of anger that block an alliance. In his workshop "The Diagnoses, Assessment, and Treatment of Clients with Anger Problems," he describes five such aspects as follows:

1. **Emotional responsibility and other blame:** This aspect refers to the inability of angry individuals to take responsibility for their own emotions. The assignment or attribution of responsibility is always directed to another person or to an external event.

2. **Other condemnation:** Generally, this involves the thinking process that leads one to see the focus of one's anger as a totally worthless and irresponsible human being. Therefore, it is the other person's responsibility to change, not yours.

3. **Self-righteousness:** Most angry people feel that they are morally justified in their anger. They feel that they were wronged by another, and this leads to the feeling that justice is on their side.

4. **Cathartic expression:** Many people have been led to believe that the best way to deal with anger is to let it out. We have been taught that if we don't let our anger out, it will build up and explode in some potentially violent fashion.

5. **Short-term reinforcement:** Often, when an individual gets angry, this anger is reinforced because it leads to compliance on the part of others. In the initial or immediate sense, the angry individual gets some reward. However, in the long term, this tends to come back to haunt the angry party due to its detrimental interpersonal effect.

Another misconception about anger is that it comes from weakness. Anger has been described as the last stronghold for those who communicate ineffectively. It is perceived as a bad emotion, as well as a moral weakness. Actually, anger doesn't come from weakness. Anger is designed to create a power position. Anger allows the angry person to be one-up at that moment in the social interaction. If you remember the end of "Guy's Story" where he said, "Your rage made me feel worthless," this is what we're talking about. Most people respond to anger with a sense of guilt or shame, and this may be based on some deep-seated early experiences of feeling vulnerable around anger, violence or potential violence.

Anger can also be perceived as a way of coping when other skills are not available. It is a means of establishing self-efficacy and control in a person experiencing cognitive dissonance (confusion). It creates the false illusion of superiority. However, the consequences of the anger generally lead to a lowering of self-esteem. It is not that we should get rid of our anger. At times anger is justified. But if your anger interferes with your work and social functioning, it creates difficulties and must be channeled in a more positive direction.

One of the important attributes found in those who are capable of making rapid and positive changes is the ability to be cognitively open: the ability to be open to new explanations of problems and new ways of managing those problems. Some individuals are cognitively closed. They feel only *they* understand their particular situation, that no one else can understand and, therefore, no one can help them. On the other extreme, cognitively open individuals welcome feedback and will grasp a new behavioral-change strategy if they feel that it will help them deal more effectively with family, job and self. Sometimes it is more difficult to deal with people who tend to isolate and go inside of themselves. These individuals may let their anger build, burst and spew forth. They may be mistrustful of others. On the other hand, the individuals who are more extroverted may reach out. They may be able to develop more trust and may be open to using modalities such as self-help groups, therapy groups, or interactions with friends or therapists in a positive, constructive way. Personality factors are also critically important. Individuals with a high degree of social skills who have social interests and "sparkle" (seem to attract others) may have an easier time dealing with group or individual therapy. They also find people are attracted to them and want to help them. On the other extreme, people who tend to be a little irritable and distant do not attract people that may be of help to them into their lives. So, one way of understanding anger from the perspective of change is to understand that there are multiple variables that go into the formula of successfully managing one's anger. These include: your personality, your experience, the people you place around you, your openness to change. All are important aspects of one's potential for making positive change.

On the far side of anger is happiness. Maybe one way to understand anger is to look at its polar opposite. Dennis Wholey, in his book *Are You Happy?* reports that the experts he interviewed believed that only about 20 percent of Americans are happy. Woody Allen, in the movie *Annie Hall,* could not conceive of happiness at all. He described only two types of lives: those that are horrible and those that are merely miserable. The authors here take no such stand, but we do believe that if you look at the cosmetics industry, the clothing industry and the reliance on fad diets, many Americans are looking outside of themselves for happiness. This tells us that something is not going right on the inside. Maybe it is the lack of connectedness. Maybe the lack of spiritual essence leads us to look outside of ourselves for the answers. Americans drink, drug, eat and sexually act out. All of these behaviors are performed under the guise of feeling good. If you were to study happy people, you might find that they possess certain attributes. Many will state that they feel very much in control of their lives. Certainly people who feel out of control of their lives, such as those living in extreme poverty, those in nursing homes or those in the prison system, may lack this sense of control. They may be angry because of a perceived injustice. People who are happy usually have a good self-concept. As mentioned earlier, they often enjoy being around other people and are typically blessed with a rather optimistic outlook on the world. They believe that things will get better and that they do have some control over this process.

If we looked at the opposite side of happiness as being unhappy, dissatisfied and angry with one's position in life, we could say that the most dissatisfied and angry are those who are pessimistic, feel totally out of control of their lives and, often, have a lower self-esteem. These individuals often have thought patterns that lead them to believe that they are victims.

As mentioned in this section's introduction, the world around us often leads us to feel that things are out of control. There are so many decisions that we need to make. Very few are all right or all wrong; we are surrounded by ambivalence. We often miss the calming rhythms of life: mountains, waves at the beach, an uninterrupted day in the country. The calmness of a predictable day is typically replaced with car horns and crisis. A spiritual connection is so essential to rising above the anxiety and anger around us. And, as we try to empathize with what's happening to the world around us, wouldn't it be nice to take a moment and empathize with ourselves.

We also need other people in our lives. Just maybe "Clay's Story" summed it up the best. If you remember, Clay expects to be rejected by the dean of the school. He actually sets up a scenario that leads to that rejection. Instead, what he finds is caring, understanding and compassion in another human being.

We must not forget that there are others out there like us, people who are worthy, moral and willing to help. We have to be able to reach out to them. As Clay said, "I know that the world is not always this way, and I know there are plenty of compassionate people out there." Often, if not most of the time, the reason that we are angry cannot be fixed simply. But, somehow, to know that somebody else cares and is willing to listen and to understand is the most effective way of managing one's anger.

In section two of this book, we will talk about people who have suffered much deeper hurts. These hurts were often caused at the hands of those who should have loved and cared for them. These hurts occurred very early in their lives. In these individuals, there is a need for ways to change that go beyond just a shift in thinking or a change in behavior. Healing these hurts will involve a deeper, insight-oriented approach.

SECTION TWO

Deeper Hurts

3

Lost and Found

INTRODUCTION

In his book *On Becoming a Person,* therapist Carl Rogers writes: "We cannot change, we cannot move away from what we are, until we thoroughly accept what we are, then change seems to come about almost unnoticed."

In this chapter you will meet real people who are lost. They have tried many ways to make their pain and anger go away. They feel as if there is a hole in their soul, and when the cold wind blows through it, it hurts. Existence seems one frustration after another; positive change seems remote.

Life can be full of loss, hurt and betrayal. At times it may even feel as though God has deserted us. We lose our innocence and our friends; death shadows us; and, heaven knows, our health is a precarious commodity.

Everyone suffers. Anger and loss of trust are the results of great losses and great hurts. In the stories within this chapter, some lose their childhood while others lose close friends. Some have been angered and hurt due to the death of a family member or the discovery of a major health problem. All will take different paths home. All will find their own way back to the light. During the process, they learn to accept reality and to trust not only themselves, but others.

Although beaten up in the process of life, the people you will meet here have found meaning in the midst of chaos, and have become stronger and wiser. They've gained the capacity to face fear and frustration head-on, and are learning that life cannot be successfully lived in isolation. People need other people. By accepting others into their lives, people learn about themselves. Borrowing again from Rogers, "If I can provide a certain type of relationship, the other person will discover within himself the capacity to use that relationship for growth and change and personal development will occur." Listen to the words of John T. as he describes his special relationship with Bryan. In the first story, John tells us how his relationship with Bryan taught him about himself, helped him grow and helped him view the world in a different way.

All of us lose something of value in our lifetime. You're about to read stories of people just like yourself who have experienced a deep sense of loss. Throughout these stories their simple switch in perception becomes evident. Instead of "Why me?" the important questions become "What am I supposed to learn from this experience?" "How do I view tragedy and liability as an opportunity for personal growth?"

In this first story, John, a young man of just twenty stands by helplessly for seven months and watches his best friend die a painful, lingering death. He knows that he had to learn a hard lesson about life; he just wishes he could have learned this one in some other way. Through this ordeal, John is made to realize that Bryan was put into his life to teach him an important lesson. That lesson is courage—the courage to be the very best he can be—every day of his life. John also learns compassion, and from this, a willingness to help others.

In the story of John T. and Bryan, you will get a first-hand view of a process called grief. The grief process is a series of stages one goes through while dealing with a significant loss. In John's case, it is the loss of his best friend and confidant. There are six stages to grief. The first, which takes place soon after a traumatic event, is *shock and emotional numbing*. The second stage is *anger*. Sometimes the anger is unleashed on the world, at God or at oneself. Some of us focus on the rage and seek the hurt. The third stage is *denial*. Sigmund Freud defined denial in the 1890s as a disavowal of painful reality. Certainly, during times of great pain and anguish, our brain protects us by denying reality. *Bargaining* is the fourth stage of the grief process. In order to lessen the blow, we seek some compromise or some way of understanding our pain or loss. This helps us to reduce the full impact of the painful experience. However, the full emotional impact of this loss starts to break through and is felt in the fifth stage. This stage is called *depression*. The depression stage is like a room that is icy, cold, blue, lonely and full of pain. When we step into this room, our immediate reaction is to jump out and back into the stages of bargaining, anger and denial. However, in order to truly work through the grief process, we must experience this profound depression with all its isolation, pain and loneliness. Only by fully exploring this fifth stage can we truly accept our loss. During the sixth stage of *acceptance* I do not mean that we necessarily understand our loss; in acceptance we find meaning, even though the event defies intellectual understanding or rationalization.

Anyone who's felt the loss of a loved one can relate to John's pain as he does the hardest thing he's ever had to do: hold the hand of his friend who is barely breathing. John breaks down as the awareness hits him that he'll never see his friend again. He experiences a profound sense of depression, and the illusions he harbors, which are part of denial and bargaining, fade away. Like anyone who's dealt with profound loss, John ultimately reaches the stage of acceptance. Friends help him with their kind and unwavering support. The depression lingers on as he takes time away from school to find himself. The loss of Bryan has left a hole in John's life that must be filled.

John changes because of his relationship with Bryan. He doesn't understand why Bryan was taken away but surmises that is not for him to understand and that he needs to somehow let it go. But in coping with any traumatic event, it's important for John to remember Bryan and to continue to talk with people about this special friendship that shaped his life.

"Martha's Story" is about the loss of childhood and the loss of innocence. Martha was a victim of what can be described as "sanctuary trauma." She experiences neglect and sexual abuse at the hands of those whom she should be able to trust—her parents.

There are many kinds of trauma. Some are the result of natural phenomena such as earthquakes, floods and hurricanes. Others are man-made traumas. These traumas often involve sexual, physical and/or emotional abuse.

Each of us responds to trauma in a different way. Martha responds in a typical fashion. She experiences a sense of abandonment with a generalized lack of trust. Her view of the world as a benevolent place is changed. All of a sudden, the world becomes a place where people cannot be trusted. It becomes a place that is unjust. All that she desires is to get rid of the terror inside of her and find a place where she can be safe. In her world, when she trusts someone, she gets hurt.

When one is put in a situation like Martha's, one's concept of "normal" is changed. In a normal childhood, parents are there for us, creating fair and consistent experiences in our early life. When these experiences are lacking, we grow up to wonder what "normal" means. Our personal development is interrupted by repeated traumatic events with multiple consequences. Martha vividly describes the physical consequences of her abuse, including the physical ailments she suffered and their resulting drain on her energy.

Early repeated trauma frequently causes dissociative symptoms. These are times when we feel removed from ourselves or from the world we live in. At times, Martha doesn't know whether she's experiencing feelings from the past or the present. She strongly desires to find out how other people live and what they want out of their lives. She wants to know how it feels to be "normal."

Martha's story is about her emotional struggle to find inner peace. She desperately wants to relate to people around her in a way she describes as normal. She wants to have a relationship and to be able to have loving and caring feelings for someone. She wants to be able to trust, but her anger makes her cautious. At fifty-five, she is still moving toward these goals and striving to develop a more compassionate view of the world. She tells us not to forget the trauma she went through or the trauma that other children are going through today.

For some people, anger seems to come from a dark place. "Tim's Story" is about Tim's internal struggle. He struggles to stuff his anger and to never show anyone that it hurts on the inside. We watch him go through three distinct periods in his life. The first period involves external control. All Tim really wants to do is to please his dad. Unfortunately, this is an impossible task. In the second period of Tim's development, he enters a stage of self-destruction. When his father dies, Tim feels empty and alone. As a result, Tim enters a period of cold solitude and tries to soothe his emptiness with behaviors that are ultimately self-destructive.

There are several other factors that are evident during the first two stages of Tim's development. He feels that he can never be good enough to fill his father's shoes, and becomes self-critical and a perfectionist—the very nature that drives him to succeed. Unfortunately, no success is ever perfect; therefore it is never good enough. Tim is trying to fulfill an illusion and play out a dream. Tim's father died while Tim was young. No man can be as good as his boyhood illusion of his father.

In the third stage of Tim's development, he uses lessons he learned from his dad. His modeled behavior helps to pull him out of his self-destructive solitude. Tim becomes a workaholic—just like his father. It is his way of stuffing the rage and assuring himself and his dead father that he's okay. In Tim's family, production is everything.

During this stage, Tim's anger becomes his inner guide and motivator. He looks at his anger and sees this energy as his friend. He converts the energy to something positive. Beneath Tim's rage is a perpetual fear. The fear of not being good enough. Only when he confronts his fear does the healing occur. In Tim's case, he has a wonderful teacher—a son.

Tim's story is about his struggle with anger and bitterness, the bitterness born of being raised in a family with social prominence and position. It is a story of growing up with high expectations and the loss of self-love and confidence that go with it. Tim charts his own course, away from his family and from the anger he associates with it, and eventually learns to use his anger as a tool to motivate—not to self-destruct.

Imagine growing up with a chronic illness. Imagine that in addition to your illness, you live in a family environment in which you are neglected. Think about spending years fantasizing about having a better and different life than the one you are living.

Children who grow up in homes where neglect or other forms of trauma are present often experience a fear of abandonment. They may use impulsive behaviors such as angry acting out to get the attention they crave, and they may continue to act out throughout their lives. At first, these behaviors work to get the attention. But their caregivers, after years of coping with the negative behaviors, generally begin to reject it.

Such is the case of Alice, who is neglected early in her life. This neglect and her illness leaves her angry at the world. She views the reality of her life and compares it to what she feels it should have been like. The drastic contrast gives her feelings of rage. She longs for, and fantasizes about, a life that would be much different—a life that would include a real family, a family that would care for her and in which she could feel safe.

Alice never feels safe. Anytime anyone tries to get close to her, it brings back the vulnerabilities of her youth, and she responds with rage. Throughout her life, she has shut the world out. It is as if she hears an internal dialogue that tells her that every time she lets someone get close, she gets hurt. Her life replicates her early experiences within her family.

Alice also suffers from very poor self-esteem, and to be happy she fantasizes about a world and a life that do not exist.

Alice is learning to deal with her rage and the negativity she has about the world with the help of a therapist. Through this relationship, she learns how to trust and she learns that her life can be different. She also learns that everyone has the power to change.

A very important connection in "Alice's Story" is the internalization of a lesson. To care for and accept (trust) others, we must first care for and trust ourselves. As Alice begins to learn this, she develops patience and tolerance for others. She develops a softer side. This is not a linear process for Alice. In the long run, however, her relationships with people bring her the gifts of love and security. She gains confidence in herself and reaches out to help others. The true test for Alice begins when she suffers a second major trauma. Alice develops breast cancer and at first feels betrayed by God. Because of her newfound ability to reach out to others, she learns that "people really do the healing."

"Alice's Story" is about the loss of a normal and nurturing family life. It's about her struggle to accept herself and to be accepted by others. It's also about her search for friendship and purpose. Alice takes the slow and painful steps necessary to release herself from loneliness and from the self-erected barrier of her anger. For a long time that anger protected her. When that protection breaks down, Alice knows it is time to leave her anger behind.

In the final story of this chapter, we learn how families can sometimes live a lie. Deborah's family secret is well maintained by the "no feel" rule. Whenever Deborah feels angry, she is told not to express the emotion. She is told to behave herself and not to act out. These are very confusing messages to a child. When children feel angry and are told that they are not angry, this message does not validate their internal experience.

In families like Deborah's, anger manifests itself in its members in the following way: The pressure builds like a volcano. No one is instructed as to how to appropriately handle the anger and rage, so they act out their anger in inappropriate behaviors. As a kid, Deborah would yell and kick. She would lie on the floor, kicking and screaming. As an adult, she vents her anger in negative and destructive ways within relationships. Deborah's life seems like a roller-coaster ride as she alternates between stuffing her anger and expressing it in hurtful ways.

A telling part of Deborah's story is the statement that she makes about anger. Deborah says that anger feels like power to her and that she would much rather be angry than sad because she associates sadness with weakness. Like most people, Deborah doesn't like to feel weak. When she feels angry, she feels strong. She believes that anger works for her in the business world as a good weapon and a tool, in an expedient sense. It keeps people away and sometimes allows her to win the moment. Ultimately, her reflections reveal that her anger generally works against her.

Through some flip of perception, Deborah finally recognizes that anger is a choice. This is a critical point in her perception of her level of control over her world. Once Deborah realizes she can choose to either let the anger destroy her or strengthen her, her world changes. With this choice, she finds solitude. Anger has become a choice and not a gut-level reaction for Deborah. She then tries to take a stand to make it an ally rather than using it to injure others.

"Deborah's Story" is about the recovery of a side of Deborah that she loved but that anger took away—her compassion and softness. Her story is about the recovery of a personality that is whole and complete, not one-sided.

Take note of several of the authors' reflections as well—

especially in "One More Surprise" and "Those Who Sustain Me."
The first selection concerns a loss of innocence and the recovery
of the self. The other is about the loss and recovery of family life.
These stories illustrate how the anger of the past can be turned to
an understanding of one's personal role in family dysfunction,
and how this understanding can be used to bring about forgiveness, restoration and acceptance.

Please note that in the second section of this book, anger is
not viewed as an emotion or behavior to be judged or elimi-
nated. No one in any of these stories views anger as something
evil or wrong. Instead, they see it as a tool for their emotional
and spiritual growth, a necessary and often healthy vehicle of
expression. They provide a good balance for those who may tend
to falsely equate a sunny exterior with good emotional health.

Where Do You Shine?

Where Do You Shine?
What road is this?
What place?
What time?
What for?
It's all tangled now, all mixed
And without feeling.

Want the touch of God to touch the anger
That touch—that strange sound of love in the
darkness that so many of those "kooks" seem to feel.
The miracles in the hands of simple people;
All seems so easy,
But maybe not, maybe not.

Where do you shine when the light in your
Heart goes out—when that very small flame that
Feeds you is snuffed?

Where do you shine when the sadness, when the
Anger is deep,
And the tears won't come.

Run quickly, quickly, to your memories, and the
Promise of God for the days ahead.

—BILL CHICKERING

ONE MORE SURPRISE

Small towns have a way of hypnotizing us. They seem so safe and secure. Their green lawns, quiet streets and familiar faces keep the outside world outside.

"You are going to grow up to be like your father," they said. They would make sure everything was worked out. No worries, and no aggravations.

On a spring evening in the early 1970s, the quiet was ruptured. Two detectives came to the house and arrested me on a marijuana charge. As they led me away, I told my mother, "Don't worry. I will be all right."

Remarkably, my first sense was one of relief. Crazy as it sounds, my thought was that it was all over. All of my confusion over career, medical school and what to do with my life ended at that moment. It was like someone took all of the tough decisions from me. I was now at the will of the judicial system. Maturity could wait, I assumed, and I took off across the country in a VW microbus with a painting of "Mr. Natural" on its side. The Grateful Dead song, *Goin' Down the Road Feeling Bad* rang out from the radio.

My feelings of relief were short-lived. I faced a judicial system that seemed hell-bent on taking away my freedom. My calm was replaced by rage. I was angry at everything, about everything and for any reason. I was being screwed. Or at least that's the way it appeared to me. I was a pending notch on some prosecutor's gun.

During closing arguments, my attorney made an impassioned appeal on my behalf. I thought, *How interesting! This guy took a hit of speed prior to summation.*

As I watched the amphetamines talk, I boiled on the inside. My thoughts were, *How unfair. This is outrageous!* It certainly was not small-town politics. I had lost all innocence.

When I got home that night, there was one more surprise awaiting me. In the mail was a note from the dean of the school. It was short and sweet. It read: "Don't come back." This blow was supposed to be softened by the add-on, "May God help you find another way in life."

I understood resentment but had never felt this level of rage and desire for vengeance. I imagined myself diving across his desk and strangling the life out of him. This was the first time in my life I had entertained the possibility that I might be capable of murder. They say time heals all wounds. They also say crisis makes you either weaker or stronger. Looking back, I realize that time helps change disposition, but time alone is not enough. I had to pick myself up after losing everything and somehow start over. Time may reduce the intensity of feelings, but it takes action to turn a lemon into lemonade.

As it turns out, these events helped shape what I have become. I learned that I never wanted to pass that way again. So I worked hard to complete my education. I worked hard to establish myself in a profession. I worked hard to restore family relationships that had been shattered. Oh, and I wrote a letter to the dean. I wanted to thank him for his wish. God *has* helped me find another way in life.

JOHN T. AND BRYAN'S STORY

We are, each of us, angels with only one wing,
and we can only fly by embracing one another.

—Luciano de Crescenzo

Bryan and I met when we were in ninth grade. We had a class together, and both of us tried out for the varsity basketball team. We got the chance to know each other well that year since we both spent a lot of time on the bench. The coach reserved guys like Bryan and me for those special moments when we were ahead by thirty points and there was less than a minute left to play. So we had the chance to do a lot of talking while we were "riding the pine."

We became best friends rather quickly. After ninth grade, we took as many classes together as we could, just so we could spend time with each other. Usually, if you found one of us, you'd find the other as well. We were the target of a lot of jokes about being "attached at the hip."

During our years in high school, Bryan and I got really good at pulling practical jokes on people. We enjoyed our status as "partners in crime." I know our parents weren't too thrilled about all our pranks, but for the most part, Bryan and I had a blast.

Once I finished high school, I had plans to attend college out of state, in Alabama. Bryan and I had a talk about it, and I decided it would be tough to leave my best friend for the better part of four years. We wound up registering at Florida State and got an apartment together.

I'm pretty quiet when it comes to talking about my emotions or when I'm hurting. And even though it took a while, I began to trust Bryan enough to start opening up and talking a bit. The stronger our friendship grew, the more we could talk about the things that were really important to us. We knew we could trust each other. When my girlfriend of several years and I broke up, it was really painful for me. I'm grateful I had Bryan there to see me through the rough times I had with that.

Bryan and I were in the same classes, took trips together, and he came over to our house a lot. Over time, my mom and dad began to see him as part of the family. My mom liked to say that as long as the two of us were in the house, they didn't need to rent movies, listen to music or watch television. Bryan and I provided all the entertainment.

Bryan and I also pledged the same fraternity together—Sigma Chi. The initiation time was pretty intense, not just because of all of the crazy things we had to do, but because of some of the more serious stuff. At one point in the process, we had to sit down with another brother in the fraternity and tell our life story. I learned a lot of things about myself; both the good and the not-so-good.

Bryan was also moved during the initiation period. He even wrote his parents a letter—a very loving and honest letter. The letter reflects the essence of the Bryan I knew.

In February 1995 Bryan got sick. At first it looked like it was just a cold. But when it settled in his lungs, the doctors said he had pneumonia and kept him in the hospital for some tests. I made sure I was at the hospital every day. I wanted to be there for him; I knew he would do the same thing for me.

A short time later, Bryan was diagnosed with a rare heart and lung disease. The doctors said he would need a double lung transplant. When Bryan told me this, I didn't know what to think or how to feel. He didn't appear too upset about it.

My mom, however, knew how serious it was. She told me there was a possibility that he could die from this disease. I broke down and cried. It was the first time I ever remember crying about anything.

When it began to sink in that my time with Bryan might be limited, I got angry. I was angry with God because I just didn't understand what was going on or what God might be trying to do. I didn't understand why, and still don't.

Growing up, I used to get angry at stupid little things. I was taught at home that it was okay to be angry, as long as you didn't take it out on others. It's always better to talk it out, not take it out. Taking it out on other people doesn't help at all.

My anger was the kind that would build up, explode and then be gone. And although I was taught not to take it out on others, I can remember getting thrown out of numerous city-league basketball games because I didn't listen to that advice.

At the time Bryan got sick, we were sharing a house. Eventually, he had to move home, where he could get more care. He was having some difficulty breathing, but it still wasn't too bad. As the disease progressed, he got steadily worse and eventually had to be on oxygen twenty-four hours a day.

Bryan and I both loved to go to the movies, even after he became ill. We went in the afternoons instead of the evening because Bryan's oxygen machine made some noise and there weren't as many people there during matinees who would be disturbed by it.

It was painful for me to watch my best friend deteriorate

before my eyes. But as Bryan's illness progressed, my anger began to go away. I believe the only reason it did was because of the way Bryan was dealing with it. He felt that he would overcome it, and his attitude helped mine.

As time went on, Bryan couldn't move any further than the length of his oxygen cord. He began having heart problems, nosebleeds and even bled from his eyes. It amazes me how much courage and strength he showed. He joked a lot and maintained the same attitude he always had.

Bryan's strength and determination helped me. I continued to go over to his home every day, and we would watch television and play computer games. It was amazing. His attitude became mine. He did not think he was going to die, and at that time, I didn't feel he would either. I no longer felt that my time with him would be limited. All I knew was that he was my best friend and I wanted to be there for him just as he would be for me.

Bryan truly believed that God would not give him anything he could not overcome. In a letter to a friend, he wrote that he felt privileged that God had given him such a great challenge. It still gives me strength every time I read it.

My friend had given me a lot of strength. I didn't even think of the disease's progression that much anymore. Then one day my mom told me that Bryan's condition was very serious and donor lungs had become available.

Bryan was flown to Shands Hospital in Gainesville, where they specialized in transplants. My parents, my sister and I drove there to be with him.

It hit me that although Bryan and I were best friends and he knew it and I knew it, I had never told him how much his friendship meant to me. When I thought of how serious the operation was, I realized that there was a real possibility that I would never have another chance to let him know. I'm not that great at talking about my problems, feelings and emotions, so I wrote Bryan a letter. In it, I told him that I would always be there for him no matter what he needed or when he needed it.

I wrote the letter on September 8, 1995—the night before Bryan would leave for Gainesville. I was visiting in his room at the hospital when my younger sister, Kristen, came in. Bryan was having an awful lot of trouble breathing then, but some things still hadn't changed. He looked over at my sister and jokingly said, "Kristen, you take my breath away."

When it was just he and I in the room, I handed him the letter and told him to read it after I left. I'm thankful I gave it to him that night; I didn't know it then, but that night was the last time I would ever talk to him.

Sometimes we wonder whether we make a difference to someone or something just because we are there. Bryan's family and the doctors told me that what I had done over the past months had made a lot of difference to Bryan and had helped to keep him going. It felt good to hear that; I know how much Bryan had kept me going.

The lungs for the transplant had come in, but they could only give him one of them because the other one was infected. The first report we had after the surgery was that he was doing all right and making good progress.

It was the beginning of a new semester as well. I had only been back to classes a few days when a friend gave me a message to call my dad. Bryan's condition had worsened, and my mom was on her way to Gainesville to be with his parents. I told my dad I wanted to drive down there alone. Dad said no to that. He knew that I was distraught and thought it would be unsafe for me to go alone. I like to drive alone when I'm upset because it gives me a chance to think about things for a while. But Dad did the right thing because right about then, I was very upset.

When we got to the hospital, Bryan was unconscious. The doctors told us that although he was hooked up to a lot of machines, we should talk to him as though he could see and hear us.

I remember walking into his room. I sat next to him, held his hand and talked to him. It was the hardest thing I've ever done. He was barely breathing; it was horrible. I knew he didn't want to live like that. (Before he left for Gainesville, he told me that he didn't want to live hooked up to machines and not being able to leave a room.)

As I sat there holding his hand, I realized that both he and I were ready for whatever happened.

My family and I went back to our hotel room for the night. The next day, the doctors told us that Bryan was showing some improvement, but not much. When we got to Bryan's room, his family was huddled and crying. We went out of the room again, and for the next forty-five minutes, a steady stream of people and machines moved in and out of Bryan's room. We would hear the heart monitor start, then stop, then start again.

Then our family went to another waiting room so Bryan's family could be alone. What followed was something I will never forget. I heard Bryan's dad walking down the hall toward us. I couldn't see him, but I knew it was his dad because I heard change jingling in his pocket; I knew that the doctors weren't walking around with change jingling in their pockets. When I finally saw him, Bryan's dad was holding his wife up so she wouldn't slump to the floor.

Bryan's mom came to where I was sitting. She knelt down in front of me and told me that Bryan did not make it. I broke down, knowing for certain that I would never see him again.

You see, Bryan's attitude had been so positive right up to the end that it had strengthened me as well. Until Bryan's mom knelt down and told me, I still thought there was a chance.

His mom and I stood in his room. Then she walked out and left me to spend time alone with him. I stayed for a few minutes, then as I walked out to be with my family, I remembered that I had forgotten something. I went back into the room to the calendar on the wall. I tore off the page, folded it up and put it in my pocket—September 16, 1995.

When I returned to Tallahassee, I called friends and told them about Bryan. I went to the fraternity house and talked with a few of the pledge brothers who then spread the word about Bryan's death. Some of the brothers came to my apartment to give me support. We talked a lot, told funny stories we remembered about Bryan and laughed a lot. By the time they left, everyone felt a lot better.

At the death of a brother in Sigma Chi, we do what's known as a "white rose" ceremony. Normally, the president of the group speaks at this occasion. Our president asked me to be the one to speak instead. Naturally, I said I would love to.

The viewing at the funeral home was very hard for me, and for everyone else as well. All of the fraternity brothers were there, 120 of them. I don't think I've ever seen that many twenty-year-olds crying before.

After a while, people began to leave. Before long, it was just Bryan's dad, several of the brothers and me, standing by the casket. Bryan's dad is a big guy. We stood in a small circle, and it seemed as though his dad's arms wrapped around everyone's shoulder. We just stood there very quietly.

A few minutes later, I walked over to the casket and kneeled beside it. I began to weep; it seemed as though the tears just kept coming and coming. I don't know how long it was before I left.

All of the Sigma Chi brothers were wearing their fraternity pins. But for some reason, no one could seem to find Bryan's. That predicament was easy for me to remedy. Before they finally closed the casket, I took off my pin and pinned it to his jacket.

On the day of the church service, I spoke at the white rose ceremony. I read from our ritual book on God, our faith and our fraternity. I found that I spoke easily and without hesitation. That was a first for me. It was just one part of me that experienced a transformation because of my friendship with Bryan; I found it much easier to speak in public than I ever had before.

I was a pallbearer. As I helped carry Bryan's casket from the church, I saw a sight that made me feel wonderful inside. All my 120 fraternity brothers were there. They formed a line on both sides of us as we carried the casket down to the hearse. It was an amazing sight.

At the cemetery, I made a few closing remarks at the graveside. Then each fraternity brother filed by the casket and laid a white rose on top of it. It was a scene I will never forget.

I was a pretty good student in school. But after Bryan's death, I wasn't functioning well. It seemed as though I just couldn't concentrate anymore. I was also failing in my classes, and that was hard for me to take since I took pride in academics and in my grades.

A couple of fraternity brothers had gone through what I had. One had a girlfriend of five years die, and another had three people who were very close to him die within a short period of time. I asked them how they handled their grief. They both told me the same thing. They needed time by themselves, time to get away from distractions. They recommended I take a semester off.

I was grateful that I was able to arrange to leave school and not have to worry about my grades or my scholarship. Then I took a leave of absence from work, as well. I was on my own. I drove to visit friends at Baylor University in Texas and then to North Carolina. What I learned was that the quicker you allow yourself a chance to grieve, the quicker you can heal. Some people keep busy, but that would not be good for me.

When spring semester came around, I was ready to deal with things again. I still get sad and angry; but I believe that we all get stronger over time, and I know that things will work out for me and for Bryan's family.

I have changed because of my time with Bryan and because of his death. As I've mentioned, I am more comfortable speaking and being in front of people now. But there is something else as well. For years, I was not the kind of person who did things for other people. Because of Bryan's strength and courage, that has changed. I have become someone who does more for people and is willing to give.

And I don't worry about things as much anymore. One big reason for that is because of Bryan and his attitude about his illness; he just didn't worry about it.

I was angry for a while, but I'm not angry much anymore; and I'm not angry with God anymore. I do not understand why Bryan was taken away from me. I guess it is not for me to understand, and I need to let go of it.

I do wish I could have learned these lessons some other way. But I do know that I will see Bryan again, and I do not have any regrets. I know I did the most I could do. I still miss him a lot and think about him every day, but I know that I cannot let that consume me.

I've looked for the positives; I've had to look for them. Bryan was in my life to teach me some lessons, and I was in his to help him and be with him through the last seven months of his life. Putting this all down on paper has been difficult, but it's important for me to remember and write and talk about this special friendship as much as I can.

Thank you for letting me do this.

How Many Tears?

What is a good cry like? Is it
cleansing? Does it help any?
Does it keep you from the next time,
and from more tears?
People carry sadness, carry buckets
of tears around, that
sag their shoulders and keep them looking
at the ground.
Is there an allotment of tears? Are there
only so many we get and then our time
is up?
Do they dissipate the sadness, soften the heart?
Wrap the soul tight and keep the fear away?
Then may there be tears in my future, and more
and more rivers out of the forest.

—BILL CHICKERING

MARTHA'S STORY

Anger comes and goes with me—a lot of it goes back to when I was young. My older sister, Marcia, and I were affectionately known as "army brats." Our father was a career military man, and we traveled quite a bit—from Florida, to New York, North Carolina, back to Florida and to Korea. My father was originally from Ohio, and that was where we settled when he retired from active duty. I'm not stretching things when I say that it wasn't a very glamorous way to grow up.

The feelings I remember from my childhood are terror and the feeling of being terribly, terribly alone. My parents would go to the officer's club on the weekends and spend their evening partying, leaving me alone. When I was about six or seven years old, I'd sit in a corner of the living room so I could see everywhere and nothing could sneak up on me. I remember calling the officer's club and crying for my parents to come home—but I don't recall that it ever did any good.

Anger? I guess it's hard to say whether a little child really feels anger. Your parents are the most influential and important people in the world to you. If anything, you feel afraid. And that's what I can remember more than anything—feeling afraid.

My mother went through a lot during the time my father was in the service. He was often gone for long periods of time. I didn't know it then, but looking back, I guess that today she would be diagnosed as clinically depressed. There were long periods of time when she just seemed to be going through the motions. I also remember coming home from school and, more often than not, finding her asleep.

I spent a large part of my childhood coping with each day. I never had time to settle in and get comfortable with my surroundings. I guess you could call it a constant state of stage fright—a constant feeling that I'd be abandoned.

But I've been skirting the edges of this story, and the edges of my anger. The truth is, I'm afraid to start because I'm often afraid where it will lead. What I'm afraid to talk about is the sexual abuse suffered by my sister and me. When you're a survivor of sexual abuse, there are many times you doubt your own sanity; you wonder whether the things you discovered after years of therapy were true or are just illusions. There were several times in the past when something Marcia said turned on the lights for me and helped me know that I wasn't crazy. There's one time in particular I remember. We were having a conversation about what happened to us, when she suddenly remarked, "I tried to keep them away from you. I really tried. But I couldn't."

Every time I start to write about this or talk about it, I get angry. I'm an adult, and I don't have any problem identifying that emotion. When you're a little kid, however, and all this horror and abuse is going on around you, you don't really know what to feel. All you want to do is get rid of the terror inside you and find a place where you can be safe. The anger comes when you're older and you've had a chance to get some help. For me, the anger came when I realized that nothing I did as a little child of six or seven caused what happened with several adults whom I trusted. That's when it hit me. And that's when the healing began.

By the time I was fourteen, I was an emotional jumble. So many things were twisting around inside me that I didn't know which way to turn. I didn't have a way to understand what I was feeling. All I know is that it hurt.

So, at fourteen I started drinking. I don't want to start analyzing things, but the alcohol anesthetized my anger—and every other feeling as well. I wanted some way to numb things, and drinking worked. For a few hours, the feelings would be mercifully gone.

It wasn't until I cleaned up from the drugs and alcohol at thirty that I realized how angry I really was. And though over the last twenty-five years I've learned not to let it hurt me as much, there is still a low level of anger inside me all the time.

Why am I still angry at fifty-five? I'm angry because I lost a childhood. Many survivors of sexual abuse will tell you the same thing. I lost the chance to be playful and free-spirited—the chance to act like a kid. I had to be on guard all the time because I never knew when someone was going to hurt me again. I never knew what they were going to make me do.

I grew to distrust anything anyone in our family said. Even today, at middle-age, it's still very hard for me to trust. The message from childhood said that when you trust, you get burned.

I'm angry because I lost the chance to ever have a relationship with my parents. I lost the sense of a supportive family because mine could not afford me even the smallest sense of protection.

I'm angry because I lost a lot of years and a lot of potential. I know what I have to offer; I know what's inside me. I think a lot about what even the smallest bit of encouragement could have done. People tell me that I've done a lot with my life despite what I went through.

But none of that changes the anger I still feel because of what might have been during those years. It's time lost, and no matter which way you twist it or turn it, it's time I can never get back.

I wanted to have what I saw others have—a husband, children, a nice big wedding, weekends with the grandparents, all of that stuff.

But from the time I was very young, I knew I would never have children. I was afraid that I might do to them what was done to me. That's how I felt even though my memories were dim at the time. I don't feel that way anymore.

There are a couple of things, however, that have been harder for me to deal with than anything else. They are my biggest struggle; they cause more anger than anything else. The first are the physical consequences—the amount of energy this ordeal has sapped from my life. Various physical ailments have improved over the years but still serve as a reminder of what happened.

The second is my outlook on the world. I've had to work very hard at viewing the world as a benevolent place since that has not been my experience. Again, it's something I've basically overcome, but something that still dogs me every day. I choose my friends carefully and always will.

I feel a lot of grief and a lot of anger that my parents never encouraged me to pursue the dreams I had as a child. I am angry over the time and money that I've spent to get to a place that most people arrive at during adolescence and early adulthood. At fifty-five, I'm just reaching those stages. One of the biggest goals of my life has been to rise above the circumstances as best as I can and have what I would term a "normal" life. People often say there is no definition of normal to a survivor of sexual abuse. Things other people take for granted, such as being in touch with your emotions, wanting and having a loving and healthy relationship, enjoying hobbies and outside interests, and feeling allright about yourself are all a part of feeling normal. People who do feel normal often joke about not knowing what that is. But to a survivor of sexual abuse, it's no joke. Some days are a real struggle.

I entered the mental-health system in Ohio when I was

twenty-one. I cleaned up from alcohol and other drugs at thirty and made a commitment to therapy when I was about forty-three. So it's been quite a process. Many therapists say that if you're supposed to remember your history, you will do so when you're strong enough. It took a long time for me, but with the help of therapy, I was able to uncover memories of a tremendous amount of abuse—at the hands of three different people before the age of seven.

Then there was the isolation from my family and the feelings of being unsafe. At one point, the memories of the abuse were coming so quickly and so powerfully, and my anger was so white-hot, that I told my therapist I didn't know how I could possibly deal with that much anger and ever lead a normal life. There's that word again—*normal.*

A dozen years of talking about my abusive childhood has helped me let go of some anger. I talked about the incidents until I was so tired of talking that I didn't want to hear about it anymore. And I think it's true for a lot of people who have been through what I have and had a great deal of anger and pain to deal with. They simply talk about it until they're tired of talking about it.

I remember one especially angry moment. I had written a letter to one member of my family that had sexually abused me. I hadn't seen him in years. I simply told him what had gone on in my life because of the abuse and wondered what his response would be. In the letter he wrote back to me, he told me that he had become a Christian and had learned how to forgive others, and that it might be a good idea if I learned to forgive as well. I was furious. Not only was he dismissing me, he was using his God as a smoke screen and a justification, implying that if I were spiritual, I would find a way to forgive him. Very little makes me angrier than someone using the good and generous qualities of God and of their faith to manipulate and hurt. That's what this person did; I've not heard from him since. I've also heard of this tactic being used on others who are abuse survivors. A perpetrator conveniently "finds religion," says, "It's over now," and that's the end of the discussion.

I still feel a great deal of anger from time to time. It's not an everyday occurrence anymore, but I still feel a lot of shame about the anger I can muster up when I think about the past.

It boils down to the fact that I probably don't know what level of anger is "correct" on a day-to-day basis. At times, I don't know whether I'm feeling anger from the past or the present. I want to figure out how other people live, how other people feel and what other people want out of their lives.

The one thing that makes me angriest about my past is my pursuit today of that elusive condition—*normal.* I realize that my anger will probably not go away entirely—ever. Part of my personal growth has been to come to terms with that fact.

One the greatest gifts I've received out of this process of healing from abuse, my sobriety and working in therapy, is the clear sense of spiritual connectedness I have now that I did not have before I pursued the healing process. I believe that, in some respects, the abuse was a gift. Perhaps others might say that's just my way of rationalizing or that it's a pat and convenient answer for the abuse that I use to cover the truth and to make myself feel better.

My spiritual belief is that we choose the lessons in our lives. I believe in reincarnation and that I was meant to work through a number of hard issues with my parents—abuse being only one of them. During their lifetime, I was able to talk to my parents about the abuse and let go of them. It was an absolute spiritual necessity for me to obtain the certainty that I would not carry this into my next lifetime. I believe this strongly, and have worked with spiritual guides and directors throughout this process. My sense of the spiritual is something that seemed to evolve during the course of my life, through the healing I've experienced in therapy and through people who have been placed in my path along the way.

It was a difficult choice for me to confront my parents. My sister, who was abused, physically beaten and knocked unconscious as a child, chose another path. She believed it would be too painful to confront my parents and didn't. That was her choice—not bad, not good—just her choice. Before my parents died, my sister and I talked about the options we had if our parents should decide to leave anything to us. I told her she could have everything, which was spiritually freeing for me at the time.

Eventually, my need for closure caused me to consult a lawyer several months after my mother's death. I discovered that Mom signed the entire estate over to my sister. Even though I told my sister that it didn't matter, I guess it really did. And even though the estate was settled nearly ten years ago, it still unsettles me from time to time.

Over the course of my healing, it's been important for me to use anger as a motivator. One thought that's gone through my mind thousands of times over the years is, *Don't let them win. They've robbed you of your childhood and years of emotional health and security. Don't let them do it anymore. It's time to let it end.*

The anger has helped me set some healthy boundaries with others. It's made me cautious, not to a fault, but still cautious. One of my biggest fears is that my anger would hurt me physically over the long haul. It has, but I'm taking steps today to try to alleviate those problems. I quit smoking several years ago and have been on a rigorous exercise program for nearly three years.

I once met a Holocaust survivor. The one thing I most remember about her is how peaceful and serene she seemed to be despite the horror she had gone through in the concentration camps. I'm not really sure that people who meet me today would describe me as peaceful and serene. People have told me that I'm distant and aloof and not easy to get to know. I'm changing that, but it's taking time. I wondered when I met that woman what had helped get her to become so serene. I don't think less of myself because of the way she is, but I am curious about what she's done with her anger. Perhaps it's as simple as the fact that she's fifteen years older than I am, and fifteen years more experienced in seeing what works and what does not.

What has helped me most with my anger is my belief in a power and a purpose beyond what happens on this earth, and that for everything there is a time, a place and a reason. I think dealing with anger is a spiritual process. I have a hard time being lenient and patient with the world; I tend to be as hard on myself as I am on the world. And I'm continually suspect whenever good things happen in my life; I'm always waiting for the other shoe to drop.

I'm striving for a more compassionate view of the world. I tend to not want the world to ever forget what I've been through. As I've grown older, I've been able to let go of this notion more and more.

I do believe, however, that it is important to tell my story as many times as another survivor needs to hear it. I used to think how funny and shocking it would be to take out an ad in the local paper to tell everyone what I've been through so no one would forget.

And sometimes, even when I'm feeling good, I go back and begin to remember—not to hurt myself, but to remind myself of how very far I, and many other women, have come in our journey back. We don't deny our hurt or the anger that still lingers. It is a part of our lives, but it does not rule our lives.

What rules my life today is gratitude. Many of the dreams I never thought would come true are now mine: the dream of a happy marriage, a healthy sexuality, a hopeful view of the world, and a spiritual life that keeps me centered and alive. I have a quiet prayer I say several times a day, whenever I'm reminded of how far I've come: "Thank you Mother and Father of all the gods for the gift. I give eternal thanks for the abundance that is mine—and good things are coming to me now. Amen."

THOSE WHO SUSTAIN ME

A family elicits both the best and the worst from us. One moment we revel in its closeness and its unity; the next moment finds us wishing it would fall off the planet as soon as possible. It can cheer us with its support or bring us to our knees with its judgments.

But families, even those that seem separated and disconnected, have this remarkable ability to come together in times of crisis. The walls crumble, the lines of communication open and raw wounds begin to heal.

For nearly twenty years, my family was a blip on my radar screen. I lived in other states and was rarely home. Sometimes we'd see each other on major holidays, but not frequently. You could call us cordial and polite, but not really "close."

Eventually, my wife and I moved back to my home state. Still, my family was nearly five hundred miles away, and it might just as well have been ten thousand.

In one month, all that changed. My uncle's wife passed away. His family lived about two hundred miles north of us. Though I hadn't seen him or my cousins Eric, Kevin and Kenny for nearly twenty-five years, I went to the funeral. It was as if I had never left. My mom had already arrived to help and comfort her brother. Uncle Leroy, though he was nearly seventy-four, seemed as though he'd barely changed. He was still a passionate man, still talking a mile a minute, and still had the rebellious spirit of a young kid. Since he was a teenager, he'd loved to ride Harley Davidsons. When I walked into his garage, I saw a huge Harley touring bike parked right in the middle of everything. He still went to biker rallies in Daytona Beach and belonged to a riding club called "The Retreads." He gave me a hug that nearly broke my spine.

I was at my uncle's home for an hour or so before my cousin Eric walked in. He and I are both forty-six, and we hadn't seen each other since we were teenagers. He embraced me and simply wouldn't let go. Neither would I.

Then I found some answers. Eric and I had a common friend—alcoholism. We had both spent a lot of years in hell, watching the bottle slowly take our lives from us. I was told that before Eric and I reunited, my mom had told him a bit of my story. Now I know why the hug was so tight. As we talked throughout the day, Eric and I both discovered that we'd sobered up in the same month, just days apart, nearly eight years before.

Once we got to the funeral home, Eric took me aside and asked me whether I would be one of his mother's pallbearers. That's when the emotion began to shake me inside. I could feel the tears coming as I said, "I'd be honored." And I was. I felt the connections coming back.

I had the chance to talk with my uncle as well at the funeral home. After a brief exchange, I noticed he was standing alone in a corner of the greeting area. I have never seen a face so lost and full of grief in my life. His eyes were brimming with tears. Here was a man, a retired Air Force colonel, who had known the horror of being a combat pilot in World War II and the Korean War, and a troop and supply transport pilot during the Vietnam War. He had seen more than most of us will ever imagine, and survived.

Before we left for the gravesite, I saw him again. This time he stood at the casket, looking down at his companion of nearly forty-eight years. His eyes stayed there as the coffin was shut. I looked at his face again. The terror of three wars didn't break him, but this did.

As we gathered at my uncle's home after the service, Eric and I tried to make up for twenty-five years in a matter of a few hours. He took me aside on several occasions, and we talked, and talked and talked. We found that though we had been apart, we had walked down some of the same roads. In addition, we discovered that we had something else, something very important, in common. As he and I joked, "We both married women who far, far out-class us." Pat, Eric's wife, also took me aside to talk. She said, "Your coming here today has meant a lot to Eric. He really wanted to see you and talk to you again." Again, I felt the emotion rise up, and I felt the connection become even stronger. I knew how much I loved Joey, my wife, and I could see the same trust and love pass between Eric and Pat. He and I are both very grateful and very lucky men.

As I got ready to head out, my cousin Kevin came up and said,

"I have to go to the store. Please don't leave till I get back." Again the emotion—the connection tightening. Kevin was stationed in Okinawa with the Air Force. When he returned, I walked up to my uncle, grasped him around the shoulders and held on for dear life. We both looked at each other and said, "I love you" as I headed out the door.

I felt the connection close. Within several days of arriving back home, my wife had to be admitted to the hospital for what turned out to be nearly a month. She was in for two weeks and then had to be readmitted through the emergency room three days later.

For the entire month, I was on autopilot, trying to get some work done, visit my wife at the hospital and keep the house from looking as if it had been hit by a cyclone. I knew I would get support from my family, but I was not prepared for the outpouring of love, concern and care they showed to Joey and me. When I called my sister to tell her what happened, the first thing she said was, "I can drive down there right now if you need me to." She lives about five hundred miles away and has a wonderful husband, Tom, and two children of her own. She was willing to drop it all to come and help me with whatever I needed. I said that wouldn't be necessary. She told me that the offer still stood, however, and that I could call her anytime. Over the next month, she called two, and sometimes three, times a week just to find out how Joey and I were doing. And I called her as well. We had had our disagreements and a squabble or two over the years, but in the last couple of years, we had grown much closer in our love and respect for one another. She was there for me, and I knew she meant it from her heart. Janet, I love you, and I will never be able to thank you enough.

My mother and I had also had our disagreements and tenuous times over the years. She had often endured my long silences and infrequent calls and communication. I knew she was afraid at times that we were drifting apart, and so was I. To put it way too lightly, Mom came through like a champ. Phone calls, concern, love, flowers and warm conversation let me know without reservation that she was there and would always be there. As we spoke over the weeks of the hospitalization, I could feel much of the past melting away, and I could feel a ton of hope for the future and for our relationship from then on. I love you, too, Mom. Thanks for all the listening and for all your kindness.

And then there's my little brother, John. It's still hard to refer to someone in his forties as my "little" brother. Johnny—the renegade of the family—raising a daughter on his own and always, always, walking his own path. I know he's been carrying around his own load of heartache for quite a few years. But you never hear him say much—a "yes" or a "no," and that's about it.

My brother got on the phone one night to call and express his concern about Joey. Then he put my niece Amanda on the line. She's ten, full of fire and, as far as I'm concerned, wears a halo over her head. She played a game called "Let's goof on Uncle Bill." For more than five minutes, she had me convinced that she didn't recognize my voice and couldn't remember who I was. And I went for it like a sucker. When I heard her start laughing, I knew I'd been taken.

Johnny said much more than "yes" and "no" to me that evening. He was more animated than I had ever heard him. He wanted to know what was going on, what was wrong and what he could do. I felt closer to him than I'd felt in years. By the end of the conversation, I felt a love for him and a closeness that I didn't know was still inside me. And it went on. My nephew John and my niece Kristen, now twenty-two and twenty, called as well. Those two have always held a very special place in my heart. We've kept in contact over the years, and I've watched with great pride as they've grown into mature and thoughtful adults. My wife and I may never have children, but if we do, I would pray they grow up as John and Kristen have. They both called me during the hospitalization to lend their support and a listening ear. They will never know how much that meant to me.

John called one evening and said he was in town with a few Sigma Chi buddies; they'd be driving down to Key West the next day. I asked him to drop by, and that evening we spent four hours talking, laughing and getting really honest with each other. I shared my past, told him just how special he and Kristen were to me, and how much I appreciated him coming over to talk that evening. It became clear to me that I wasn't speaking with a kid anymore.

My father also lent his support. He'd been quite ill for some time, but he called just to let me know he was thinking of us and to ask us whether there was anything he could do. He's been there for me and has consistently supported and encouraged me in my career choices, even when I didn't want to listen or thought I knew better.

There were two gifts that came out of all of this. The first is that my family and I got a lot closer to one another. As we shared time on the phone together, inevitably the conversation would drift back to the past. We would reminisce, talk about the good times, and share the hard times with a detail and depth I had never experienced before. We opened up about the struggles and the problems each of us currently face. We confided in one another and asked each other for help and advice. I think we all began to understand that life is much too fleeting, and our lives much too precious, to hold back from one another. We spoke about what it's been like these past twenty years. We talked about what we've learned, how much we've grown and how far we have yet to go. I was dumbfounded by how much I didn't know and how much I had kept each of them in this little box of awareness that I had sealed up back in 1975. Had we been angry at one another over the years? No doubt about it. Had we done things that hurt each other? Yes, we had. Will we get angry and upset at each other in the future? We're human, so I imagine we will.

The second gift I received, I received from my wife. She recently lost both of her parents within eleven months. The losses were hard to take and still hurt her very deeply. And even though our love for one another is very strong and goes very deep, she still felt alone and left behind at times. She recently told me how much she enjoyed spending time with my family, how she felt welcomed and loved. After her return home from the hospital, she told me how much all the cards, phone calls and genuine concern from my family had meant to her. With tears in her eyes, she said that she felt part of a family again; she knew she wasn't alone.

Reconciliation: You wipe away the tears, patch up the wounds, forgive and come home again. It doesn't mean you'll always agree with one another, and it doesn't mean you'll always see eye-to-eye on everything. What it means is that where a family is concerned, the whole is greater than the sum of its parts. It means that when conflict comes, you get together and honestly seek what's best for one another. You do what it takes.

This past year has taught me a lot about myself, and even more about those folks I shared a roof and meals with for more than twenty years. They are my family, each of them different, irritating, special, compassionate, gifted and full of life in their own unique way. I am proud to call them my family. And now there is an added dimension.

I am proud to call them my friends.

TIM'S STORY

Where I grew up, it was all about style, grace and manners. If you were polite, that meant everything—even if you hated someone's guts, you were polite. And most important, you never asked any questions.

But in the fall of 1967, I asked a very important question. It was raining that day, and I was in the family car, getting ready to head off to college. I didn't have a clue as to why I was going away. That's just what was done. You grew up, swam at the country club and water-skied on the lakes. If you were a guy, you also worried a lot about overcoming your sexual shyness. When I was fourteen, I went out with three other guys. We had managed to get ahold of some Colt 45 malt liquor because someone told us there was more alcohol in it.

While we were drinking it, we loosened up and began to talk. A lot of the talk was about all the women we had been with (as if we really had). I look back on that experience now as pivotal. We learned how to lie and how to tell a tale.

Even if things weren't good at home, it all looked pretty and neatly wrapped with all the trappings of Southern hospitality— the social graces, the manners, the "good life." When your life was in total chaos, the trappings helped you keep a gracious exterior. You never let anyone see you sweat; you never spoke ill of your spouse or your family. Instead, you spoke in clichés: "How are you?" "Doing just fine, thanks. And how are you?" "Oh, I'm just fine, too."

Two things typified my home life—alcoholism and stuffed rage. That's because we couldn't talk about either of them.

But there were moments when the rage escaped. I remember being five years old. My little sister and I were sitting beside each other one evening in an upstairs bedroom. It was so dark that we could not even see one another, but I remember the feeling of our two legs touching. I also remember that she reached over to hold my hand. Both of us were very, very afraid. Through the darkness, we could hear our parents fighting downstairs. They were screaming horrible obscenities at one another—words of absolute anger and hate.

I think it was at that moment that I learned to deal with anger and rage. I learned that it should only come out at night. It should only come out when others cannot see it. It should only come out in ways that keep it secret. To this day, whenever I am around rage, anger or potential violence, I feel once again like that five-year-old. I want to go into a dark room with my little sister and hide. We can protect each other there.

For most of my life, I have vacillated about how I dealt with my anger, especially in interpersonal relationships. I've wavered between trying to control it and just letting it out. During my career, I have always volunteered for crisis teams. And if someone started losing it or went into a rage, I would always be the first in the room. It was almost as if I could control a particular situation or someone else's anger, then it would wipe the slate clean, or at least even things up.

During those crisis situations, I remember feeling as if the anger in the room was my fault. I felt responsible for it, even if there was no way I could fix it, control it or make it go away. When I was eight, I was in a club called the "Boozies," and it seemed appropriate. My friends and I all had alcoholic dads, and we took it out on our mothers and ourselves. I also played in a football league back then, as well. I was the smallest on the team and played middle linebacker. I can remember the satisfaction I got, running headfirst into a much larger ball carrier and literally knocking myself out to make the tackle. It was as though if I could just hit someone hard enough, I could somehow get rid of the anger and rage that lived in me.

But it always seemed to come back.

Let me go back to that rainy fall day in 1967. I can still picture it as if it were yesterday. I was with my mother and father and sister on the way to college. We were pulling into the driveway of the college dormitory where I'd be living. I remember thinking, *What am I doing here? I don't belong here at all.*

I didn't want to be there, but it sure beat the hell out of the alternative, which was Vietnam.

It was the spring of my freshman year when it happened: my father died unexpectedly. It was like when you're cruising along on a pleasant spring day, the windows are rolled down, the wind is blowing through your hair and you're feeling perfect. Then you're blindsided. The wind stops, you suddenly hear the screech of tires, then a crash. That was how I felt the day my father died.

I entered into a period of cold solitude. I had lived my whole life trying to please my father. Through high school I got only three B's; the rest were A's. But somehow it never seemed to be good enough for Dad. Even though I tried to do everything right, I never seemed to be able to get his attention. At one point, I even considered the ministry. But then I chose the inevitable— medical school. I did all of this to make him proud and to show the world that our family was okay. He was the town hero. He saved lives, and now he was gone. Now, who would save my life?

I felt absolutely alone when my father died. I remember coming home from school. All the townspeople were there. I remember that several adults gave me the shingle from my dad's medical office. They asked whether I wanted to use the office when I finished medical school and came back to town to practice.

When I heard that offer, something ripped in me because I knew I could never follow in his footsteps. I never, ever had been, and would never, ever be, good enough.

So then I checked out; I shut off. It was as if I'd been anesthetized. I turned on the numbness and felt nothing. For me it was a safe alternative to the rage and anger. Over the course of the years, I learned to do this very well.

Anytime I'm criticized, that numbness comes back. If, in my interpersonal relationships, someone said something to me that felt negative, I would numb out. Then I would find a way to blame them for my problems. One time my wife was trying to get close to me. She was trying to tell me how she felt and some of the ways she was hurt by my actions.

My response to her was rage and anger. I pushed her away and then numbed out again. I felt nothing at all inside—all I saw was the darkness. First light, then darkness; light, then darkness. I would spend two decades of my life struggling from the darkness to the light. There was a place inside me where I stuffed all the rage and anger, stuffed it so I wouldn't have to look at it anymore. The problem with that, however, is that the anger always manages to sneak up on you again. Just when you think you have it made, out it pops again.

My father's dead. Why? I went through a period of numbness, but that soon changed. It was as if I were gripped by darkness. I'd spent all my time trying to be good, attempting in some way to get over feelings of inferiority and self-doubt.

When my dad died, all the doubt hit the surface. So did all the anger. *I'll never be good enough. No one gives a shit about me.* I remember sitting in my college advisor's office at the time. He asked, "What's going on?" I said, "I'm great. Couldn't be better." I fooled him; I guess you can fool some of the people some of the time.

But how do you fool yourself? I tried to, but I couldn't. So I ran as fast as I could away from it. One way I did that in college was to set myself up to fail. I remember having a final exam scheduled in economics. Instead of going to that exam, and others, I took a road trip to Florida that I barely remember. I was drunk for four days. I remember being someplace in Georgia and then buying little kids carnival rides in Florida.

Some of my buddies were there with me as well. And I don't know how, but I remember we ended up someplace where we didn't belong; for me, though, it seemed to fit. I fancied myself a Robin Hood, helping out the less fortunate. In reality, however, I think it was just the darkness playing itself out. I had hair down to my waist, earrings and a pretty well defined rebellious streak.

I didn't go home much during all that time—maybe once a year. During one of those visits, I remember sitting down at a table with my mother and sister. Mom asked me what I was going to do with my life. I told her to get off my back and leave me alone, that I didn't respect her anyway. Years later I can still recall those painful words I spoke to her back then.

I remember a lot of drinking and drugging. I remember a farmhouse outside of Washington, D.C. It was there that I did cocaine for the first time and thought, *Where have you been all my life?* It was the first time I'd felt whole.

During those drugging years (in my twenties), I completely alienated my family. I also maintained a lot of long-distance romances and never let anybody get really close. I was afraid that if they did get close, they'd find out what I was really like and wouldn't want to stay around me. Long-distance romances allowed me to control the action; I could get as close as I wanted or hide completely.

I picked up a habit from my father—workaholism. In my twenties I was working sixteen-hour days, six or seven days a week. I remember sitting at O'Hare Airport. I had the flu. I was perspiring and had a fever, yet I was going to Houston to speak at a conference. I laugh just thinking of the absurdity.

I had no life but work. If people asked me about my life, all I could talk to them about was work since I was working eighty hours a week.

And I still kept trying to control things. I went back to school and majored in psychology, hoping I could help others and myself at the same time. As part of the curriculum, we had to go to a personal growth class for a year. During one session, the group listened to me attentively, then one of them said, "You know, you don't have to be this way."

I felt exposed. The game was up; no one in the group was buying what I was saying. Something in me couldn't buy it anymore either. I knew that all the money and degrees, sexual conquests, and cars and homes would never make me lovable.

A horrible picture came to my mind. I was in my eighties, sitting in a house. I was alone, having no one around, yet not wanting it that way. I was in a trap; I needed to be with people but was afraid to let anyone close. It brought me to the point where I felt suicidal. The rage pressed against my chest, and the tears welled up in my eyes. The only way I knew to deal with it was to keep running.

I eventually wound up in therapy. One of the things the

therapist told me was that I already had everything I needed. A friend of mine told me that if I just stopped running, I'd find that everything I was looking for was already inside me. He said I was okay just the way I was. He said peace of mind and serenity could be mine; all I had to do was sit still.

That was a novel concept. For so long I thought if I could just run hard enough, I could find it. There were times when if I saw someone else had it, I could get close enough and maybe learn from them. I once took a road trip to New Mexico and ended up in a Native American sweat lodge. I participated in the sweat lodge for two days; I felt cleansed. I started to feel some of the stuff inside going away.

You couldn't really say that the changes were of the cosmic, intense variety. I once heard a story about a guy who tried transcendental meditation, along with everything else, to try to overcome the problems in his life. After TM he thought he would have dreams of soaring over the world like an eagle, feeling complete release. But instead of dreaming he was an eagle, he dreamt he went to school in his underwear. That's the way I felt.

Something was happening, and like my TM friend, it was something I couldn't quite understand. I knew what I was searching for—I wanted to look in the mirror and like what I saw. I wanted to feel whole. I wanted to replace the darkness.

One evening, I was taking a walk with my young son. He was holding my hand tightly. He looked up at me and asked whether I was afraid. I told him, "No, Son, I'm not afraid." Then he let go of my hand and said, "Then I'm not afraid either." Somewhere along the way you just have to let go and trust your higher power. You have to say, "Life is worth living, so let's live it." Life is full of ups and downs, and I have two choices: I can beat my head against it or just ride with it.

Today? Well, I'm still struggling with anger and fear of intimacy and with receiving criticism. I've still got a bit of distance to travel, but I'm not as fearful anymore. As I look back on my history, I think fear was at the core—fear that I would never be good enough, fear that I could never make it.

Fear was my worst enemy, but I've made it my friend by addressing it and talking to it head-on. I've made it my inner guide and motivator, and it's helped turn my life around. In many ways, I think a small child can teach us a lot. They are totally dependent on others, yet they courageously reach out to the world at the same time. I know now that I must reach out to the world and be more vulnerable. I understand that.

I also understand that there are cherished moments in every day. For example, I know that when I get home tonight, my son will come around the corner as fast as he can, screaming, "Daddy, Daddy!" That is a moment I've lived for my whole life. In the past my fear and self-loathing would have prevented me from enjoying it.

But today I can.

ALICE'S STORY

Most of my early life was filled with loss and betrayal. I grew up in a large family in which there was a lot of abuse and neglect. There was never enough attention to go around, and as a young child, I felt lost and fearful most of the time.

I didn't talk much, and I really didn't do a great deal either.

I was sick during a lot of my early childhood. I had hyperthyroidism that went undetected between the ages of three and eight. During those five years, I felt tired and weak most of the time, and whenever I could, I slept. I wasn't able to jump around and play like all the other kids I knew.

Until adulthood, I didn't fully realize the amount of loss I went through as a child. That's just one of the losses I feel angry about—angry because it was something I had no control over. It was a loss that affected me for a long time. The first time I remember feeling anger and rage was in early adolescence. It got to the point where the anger was so great that I began to be a problem for everyone around me. And I wasn't always certain of just what it was I was angry about. I just knew I was unhappy and knew that most everyone around me irritated me.

I longed for and fantasized about a life that would be much different, a life that would have included a real family that did things for each other and cared about one another—a family and a home that felt loving and safe. I longed for friends and other joys of life that I just never had.

I just knew I was mad. I would be either very silent and withdraw from the world, or else I would lash out. At times, I would hit my brothers and sisters and neighborhood kids, and attack them in a rage. I was often upset with teachers at school. I didn't get physical with them, but I often lost control verbally.

Most people have some kind of internal control over what they say. I didn't. I'd say things to people that most people wouldn't dare utter.

Basically, I just didn't care. I was so angry and so unhappy that I just didn't care. Most people were afraid of me—even my family. They would get upset at me because of my anger or else lash out at me to defend themselves. People in general just avoided me whenever they could.

My brothers and sisters would often tell me that my anger was responsible for the way Mom and Dad acted. There were times when I felt I had to behave because our father was a very abusive man, and one angry person in the family was enough. I don't remember very many peaceful days in my home.

The neglect in our family was widespread. Food was provided, but we never felt like we could eat as much as we wanted. I don't remember being taught any basic social skills at all. Through it all, my anger just kept building and building.

I knew that what was going on with me was not normal, but because it had been going on for such a long time, I never really felt I could change, never really felt I had a choice about changing.

The only thing that seemed to dissipate my anger was pot. It put a lid on the rage. It helped me drift into a fantasy world where life was always happy and life as it was in reality did not exist. In this fantasy life, I also lived in a family that got along, wasn't abusive and treated each other well.

But the pot didn't work for long, even though I kept using it. I remember that in college people were still fearful of me. I got a lot of silence and a lot of angry looks. I still didn't like people, and I would punish them if I didn't like them for some unfounded reason or if they spoke to me when I didn't want them to.

The source of all my anger began to get less and less clear to me. I increased my use of pot until I was literally smoking it all day long. But no matter how much I smoked, it didn't seem to work. People were still very wary of me and were careful before they tried to approach.

My life got really messy. I was sad and lonely and lost. I had no straight friends anymore, only people who used drugs. And since the pot didn't seem to work anymore, I turned to food to try and smother the anger. Neither of them worked.

I finally went into a treatment program to get off pot, and I've been straight for quite a few years now. But it wasn't until I got some individual treatment and therapy that I felt any relief from the anger. The individual therapy focused a lot on my childhood and my reactions to the abuse and neglect in my family. I learned just how much all that went on in my past had cost me emotionally.

Therapy was a long and very difficult process. The therapist I worked with for the first three years helped me the most. This person cared about me, and I could feel that. And for the first time in my life, I really felt as though I could trust someone. Because of this bond of trust, I was able to take the first positive steps toward working on my anger.

As I said, it was a long process. I often resisted discussing my anger. It was just very hard for me to acknowledge how my anger had affected others and myself. Now that I look back, I can see that shame played a big role in my resistance as well. It was hard for me to see what my actions had caused and the hurt I'd caused others.

During this period of therapy, I wasn't physically abusive to people anymore, but I could still be very harsh and critical. I just didn't know how to get close to people; others sensed that, and they stayed away. Inside I really loved and cared about people, but I also knew that that was not the part of me people saw. It was only when I began to care about myself that I began to connect with other people and could begin to let go of the past. My pain and anger began to lessen. I knew that my childhood had had a profound effect on me, but I also knew that staying in the past was not helping me move on.

I got more involved in the present and tried to deal with my anger directly. I took responsibility for my actions; no longer did I give myself permission to hurt people. And I started understanding that gratitude needed to play a more important role in my life. One of the gifts I was very grateful for was my counselor. She was able to see through my defenses. She cared about me, watched over me and let me proceed at my own pace. Eventually, I was able to receive her gifts; and because I was, I could begin to give the same gifts to others and myself.

Life can be different, no matter how severe the neglect or abuse you or I have experienced. We have the power to change, and we have the power to give to others. I was amazed at the change I saw in myself over time. I began showing patience and tolerance for people. The more I was able to do that, the more I was able to step away from my past and from the anger that came out of that past.

As I continued my therapy and attended more and more recovery meetings, I found I had friends I could count on and friends who could count on me. It made a big difference because healing took place in another area of my life—relationships.

In my early thirties, I left a long-term relationship that was stable and meaningful, and entered into another relationship that I thought offered a lot of hope and would give me what I wanted. I really thought that God was rewarding me for all I had missed in the past.

But it turned out a lot different than I expected. Ending the first relationship was still the right decision, but I lost someone who had accepted me just as I was for a long time. The new relationship ended with feelings of loss and betrayal. I had given a lot to this relationship; I'd worked hard at it. When it ended, I went into a deep depression. I had thought that if you worked hard on yourself and did the right things, good things would happen. The end of that relationship rocked that belief, though over the last few years, I've been able to pick up bits and pieces of it again.

While the relationship wasn't the gift I thought it would be, it did help me to realize that I needed other people, and needed to let friends help me and be there for me. And they were. Also, I began to see my anger as a gift, as a guide to changes that needed to occur. It was an indicator that I needed to treat myself well and no longer be willing to accept injustice or mistreatment from anyone else.

After some time, I was able to enter into another relationship that is bringing me the gifts of both love and security. I am able to take confidence and hope from this relationship, and I even feel as though some of my dreams are beginning to come true.

Before long, however, I was faced with another real challenge to my belief system. I was diagnosed with breast cancer. It has been nearly two years since I went through my surgery and chemotherapy.

I was happy, I was well on my way—and then the diagnosis came. Anytime you get a piece of news like that, you immediately think about the possibility of death—the end of all your dreams and plans. It also brings up a lot of anger. And for me, a lot of questions as well: What will dying be like? What will the sickness be like? How difficult will it be for those who love me to watch me go through this?

I was scared—scared of dying and scared of the radical mastectomy and chemotherapy I was told I would need. How would the aftermath of surgery affect my emotions and my sexuality? I had never really contemplated losing a part of my body. And although these were real fears, they paled in comparison to the fear of the illness spreading and of my possible death. I went through denial, minimizing, anger and then slowly back to reality.

I got angry with the medical profession as well. I didn't get to see the oncologist I wanted because she was too busy. After I found the lump in my breast, I went to see our family doctor and was told to wait until after my next period to come in—that she didn't really think it was anything, probably a cyst. When I visited her, she made an attempt to get the fluid out but was unsuccessful. So she scheduled a mammogram, and my fear increased. I was told I needed a second mammogram and an ultrasound. They found a second lump and saw some very small calcifications as well. I was still told it was probably a cyst and that there was no need to rush a biopsy. Both the doctor and I were going to be on vacation for a couple of weeks anyway. When she and I got back, I had the biopsy, and the doctor told me it was probably not cancer.

When the pathology report came back, however, she told me it was cancer in the lump and surrounding tissue. I was numb and angry at the shock of hearing that. I just didn't even know what to think. I met with the surgeon and was told that a mastectomy was recommended in order to check and see if the lymph nodes were involved. She told me that I would also have other treatments after surgery.

Then I had to deal with the managed-care system. I tried to make appointments and schedule tests. I tried to be assertive and take care of myself, and found that people really didn't like that a lot.

I realized that as far as the system was concerned, I didn't really matter that much. They dealt with a lot of people, and to them, I was just another body. I found out that unless you were in a position of power or else had a lot of money, it was hard to get people to jump on things right away.

I wanted the surgery, and I wanted the reconstruction that would follow. It was painful to wait, knowing that there were tumors growing inside you, and not knowing whether they were spreading or how fast they were spreading. The people around me also had a difficult time, knowing what was going on, and it became difficult for me to manage both my feelings and theirs. I just got very quiet, while the people around me were a lot more verbal with their anger. Their anger disturbed me because that was not the way I wanted to deal with the illness.

I read up on cancer but still felt powerless because there was so much I didn't know. I had a load of questions, but nothing to really comfort me. After the surgery, the oncologist talked with me about the severity of my case. I was told the lymph nodes were involved and that I would need chemotherapy. The chemotherapy would present its own problems because of its side effects, which include nausea, hair loss and possible heart damage.

I switched oncologists and felt much more comfortable with a new doctor. He was more positive and let me ask a lot more questions. I kept up the chemo every three weeks—all the time feeling angry and frightened. I felt like I had already paid a lot of dues in my life. I just didn't feel this was fair. I had been feeling really good the last five years, and now this! I felt betrayed by God again.

It's now been nearly two years since the chemotherapy, and two and a half years since the diagnosis and initial surgery. A lot of my anger has diminished because I know I met the challenge and survived.

During this illness, I got to feel the love of many people, which is more healing than you know. It's the greatest healing power I know of. I am now very much involved in my life again, and I really feel I have beaten it. I'm back in school and helping others. I know today how much I want to live and just how many gifts I've received.

But people really do the healing. My friends stayed with me, my family was beside me and my partner stayed with me through all of this. Anger is still a part of my life, and I get irritated from time to time. But I deal with it differently now because I have the gift of simply being alive today. Sometimes I still snap at people, but not nearly as much as before. Joy is much more a part of my life than anger. Today, I can acknowledge the injustices in my life and in the lives of others, and do something about them. Today, my anger spurs me into action to make things better for others and myself.

That's certainly a lot better than what I used to do with it.

FISHERMEN

My son and I are fishermen. We catch the big ones— generally between three and six inches long. But to him it is a marvelous conquest. Me? I just like watching him.

At night we tell fish stories. His favorite is about a fish so large that if you hooked him, he would pull the boat all around the lake and it would take a really strong person to pull him ashore. Of course, this fish is way out in the deep middle of the lake. We only fish from the dock.

One Sunday morning my son says, "Dad, we have to get a boat." We check the newspaper for sales, and sure enough, Wal-Mart has a sale on flat-bottom boats.

When we get to the store, my son climbs into the shopping cart. I am sure all of you with children have had the experience of propelling your child around a store in a cart.

I do well and soon find the sports section of the store. Soon, we see fishing gear. My son grabs an oar and starts to row the shopping cart. As he does so, he sings, "Row, row, row your boat . . ." I am working hard on being less stuffy and adult-like, so, with some embarrassment, chime in with him.

In a corner of the fishing department, two young children start to sing, and soon a mother joins in: "Row, row, row your boat . . ." Pretty soon we have an incident in the fishing section at Wal-Mart.

Not being able to escape the fact that I am forty-seven years old, singing "Row, row, row your boat" with my son and three total strangers, the following thought grabs my mind. What if it were just me in the fishing section of Wal-Mart with an oar in my hand, singing "Row, row, row your boat"? People would distance themselves from me as if I were dangerous—or at least psychotic. Isn't it amazing how our perception of an event shapes the way we relate to it? We have, in our minds, the ability to make a lemon or lemonade out of most life situations.

DEBORAH'S STORY

When I was growing up, in my family we were not allowed to express anger. We were taught that if you were angry, you expressed it "appropriately." Whenever I got angry, I was told, "Behave yourself" and "Don't act like that."

But even though I tried to behave and keep the anger inside, there were times when everything would build and build, and I simply couldn't hold it in anymore. Then I would throw tantrums. I can actually remember lying on the floor, kicking, screaming and yelling because I wanted something that I wasn't getting. That was the only outlet I had for anger because I couldn't express it any other way.

As I grew older, as far as anger was concerned, I was told that young ladies didn't behave that way. So I didn't. I simply wouldn't recognize anger as an emotion anymore. During my teenage years, the only people I can remember sometimes getting upset at were my parents.

All through my twenties, I really did not express anger at all. And, of course, when you don't express anger, it often comes out in other ways, as it did with me. I would get sarcastic and sometimes vicious with people. I really didn't know what was going on. I had a large mixture of feelings inside me, and I didn't know what was what. Was it anger? Was it resentment? I just didn't know. It would get crazy sometimes.

During my twenties, I had a long-term relationship with a man who taught me a lot about anger. If something happened that upset him, he would just suddenly explode. I'd be scared to death, thinking, "Oh, my God. What happened?" But for him it would be over—literally. I was amazed that someone could do this. It actually taught me a pretty simple lesson—that if I was angry, it was okay for me to express it. It helped me to be around someone who didn't get uncomfortable when I got angry.

And we got angry with each other as well. Sometimes the anger was healthy, and other times it came out in negative and destructive ways. But anger, for me, has been like a pendulum: I go through periods of never being angry, just stuffing it, to periods of being angry all the time.

When I was in that long-term relationship, I would not only get angry at him, I would also get angry at work. My career was very important to me, and I was determined to make it. If anyone did anything at work that I perceived as a threat, I would go ballistic on them in very inappropriate ways, right in their face. And I didn't care.

Every time I think about being angry, I can remember those nights, laying in bed and going over my day at work. I'd think of all the things people "did" to me and just get enraged. My stomach would get in a knot, my teeth would clench and I'd stay awake, plotting how I would get my revenge.

Everything felt like a threat to me. I was just living in a constant state of rage. That was also a time in my life when I began hitting the bottle. I began to have what I call "rage blackouts." I'd have screaming arguments with my supervisor at work and, later on, not remember a thing I'd said. But the guy liked me because he had the same type of personality. We'd scream and rage at each other at work, and people would just sit around and watch. Afterward they'd tell me, "God, you were great," and I didn't even remember what I'd said.

I was a fighter with that guy. I'd get in his face and say, "Screw you! You are not going to get one inch on me."

But all this rage and anger really ate me up. It was exhausting and destructive, but it was the way I lived for years. And I was still riding that pendulum, going from always being angry and full of rage to shutting it down completely.

I learned about the proper use of anger when I got into a recovery program. Alcohol buries feelings, including anger, for many people. But that's not the way it worked for me. What alcohol buried for me was not my anger, but my softness and compassion. I was a raving maniac when I was drinking, and I was angry most all the time. Everybody made my angry. My anger was so bad at times that I was even afraid of it myself. I certainly understood my capabilities and so began to understand how people could get so mad that they could kill one another. There were times when I even remember thinking, *Thank God I don't have a gun anywhere around.* It's true. I felt that freaked out, that insecure and that threatened most of the time. I knew enough not to have any weapons around me.

I took everything personally. I thought that if people were doing something I didn't like, they were doing it to me. Then, when the anger subsided a bit, I'd sit back, amazed and think, *I was thinking about killing someone over that?*

I was in recovery from alcoholism when I decided to quit smoking. Boy, now there was some serious anger! When I was trying to quit smoking, I'd wake up in the morning, just seething with anger. And the first thing I thought was: *Who can I kill today? I am going to kill some unfortunate soul, so who is it going to be?* It was like that for the first year after I quit smoking—just pure, raw anger.

I was angry at the whole world during this year. I was also

married at the time. One day my husband came home from work, and I said to him, "You know. I hate you. I really, really hate you. I hate everything about you—who you are and everything you do. I just hate you!" And I meant it. I really meant it.

Anger is something I've never learned to deal with in a straightforward way. I skew it. I twist it. I feel it. I want to analyze it away because I am still afraid of it and know I can still do a lot of harm with it.

I know that I have damaged relationships because of my anger, but I thank God I don't get as angry as I used to. Now, I laugh at a lot of the things that used to upset me. Traffic, however, still gets me angry from time to time. People are out there in those cars, doing a lot of stupid things. Sometimes I could swear they're trying to kill me. I am amazed at how driving down the interstate can evoke such deep anger in me, and while I may say someone is trying to kill me, I know that's not really true. Some people just get on power trips when they get behind the wheel of a car.

The traffic where I live is very heavy most of the time. And when you're out there, you can just feel the aggression that some people pour into their driving. I can feel it coming at me, and I get aggressive right back. Then I tell myself, *Now, Deborah, calm down. Do you really want to end your life over something this trivial, because you got upset and got into a car accident?* But anger feels like power to me. And I would rather be angry than sad, because when I'm sad, I feel wimpy, I feel weak. And I don't like to feel weak. When I'm angry, I feel strong, and I like that. I really like that.

I remember walking into corporate board meetings angry and staying angry throughout the meeting. Anger was a good weapon there, a good tool. It made me feel strong and kept me from feeling intimidated by anyone in the room.

What I've found in business, however, is that anger will almost always work against you. If you get angry in a business situation, men don't like it. In the corporate world, men are threatened by a woman who is high-ranking, but they will accept you if you are up there and still act like their perception of a woman as someone who will not challenge them.

I was usually angry in those meetings because I was fighting for things I believed in, and I took the fight right to the men in the boardroom. I challenged them in an angry way—after all, they did that to one another all the time. But I wasn't mimicking them; I was just being myself.

That worked against me. Men are a lot happier if you come to their office crying. If you are in their office and angry, they get uncomfortable. In fact, they can't wait to get you out of their office.

There are some men, however, who are exceptions. I have been able to argue with some men in the corporate world and generate mutual respect. But to most men, an angry woman is a scary thing. Overall, I have suffered some consequences in my career because I got angry. That's because I will not compromise my ideals or values, nor will I stop fighting for things I believe in.

I have also grown a lot in how I respond to anger. Today I'm not really afraid of people's anger. When I was growing up, I was afraid of anger, especially my father's. When I was married to someone who was angry a lot, I thought that if I showed fear, he would have power over me and be able to manipulate me. So my response was to fight back.

I very rarely let people manipulate me with anger, especially in the business world. If people are angry and they want to talk about it, that doesn't bother me, because I'm not afraid of their anger, unless the anger should start to get physical. When I started my last job, I thought, initially, that it was a good fit. What ended up happening was that I was betrayed by people I thought were friends, people I had trusted and, in several cases, had even promoted to higher levels of job responsibility.

The people who love and care about me are angrier about this than I am. I think one of the reasons for that is that I know if I let myself get too angry about it, I would just get eaten up inside and not be able to move on or concentrate on taking the next step in my career. I'm trying to look at it from a different angle these days. I want to see the blessing and the opportunity in what has happened. Frankly, I just don't want to waste energy on the people who sold me out. I'm really proud of myself because I did not waste all that emotion. But I am angry at myself for not seeing it coming. I realize now that several people had an agenda all along but that I just didn't know it, or was so busy that I was unaware of it. Then I started to mistrust myself for not being a good judge of character and wondered, *How can I ever have another person work for me? I won't know whether they're being real or not.* What finally pulled me out of all of that self-anger was realizing that if I kept ripping myself to shreds, I was just letting them win. I've tried to take my power back and not live in a spirit of revenge. I don't want to live with tension and with knots in my stomach. I used to live like that all the time when I was drinking, and, at times, I was suicidal.

I guess that in a lot of cases anger is a choice. That's the way it was with the betrayal at work that cost me my job. I can choose whether I'm going to let it destroy me or strengthen me. Initially, I found peace in solitude, and then I reached out to some friends for help. In this case the process of letting go of the anger has been ongoing as more information keeps getting revealed to me about what actually went on. I have to continually reaffirm my stance to let it go. Not getting what I want also makes me angry; so does people not treating me the way I think they should. And this side of me comes out even stronger in a love relationship than it does in business. I think this happens a lot with people in intimate relationships because it is in this type of setting that we make ourselves the most vulnerable. Our very essence can be threatened if something goes wrong, or if we feel the other person has hurt us or violated our trust. Today I know what I have to work on: I have to soften my tongue and work hard on watching what comes out of my mouth. I have a hair trigger at times, but I consider that a good thing because it's protected me on a number of occasions. I believe the pendulum has not swung back to the middle yet, and maybe it never will.

But at least I have access to my anger as a tool for survival. And I can ask myself some probing questions when my anger does begin to rise: Is this legitimate? Is this something I should pay attention to? Is this worth my time? Or am I just being a spoiled brat? Honestly answering those questions will help me evaluate my anger more carefully and listen to the anger while not letting it injure others.

Trusting the Process

INTRODUCTION

Patience and time do more than strength or passion.

—La Fontaine

It's often hard to understand or believe that the hard times and disappointments we experience in life are part of a process. For this reason many of us, rather than trust that growth takes time, succumb to the fashion of the times and try to rid ourselves of anything that doesn't feel comfortable or pleasurable. We've learned to view hardship and struggle as signs that something is wrong—if we can't fix it quickly, there's something lacking in us. What's amusing, however, is that when we look back on our past, we often say, "I wouldn't have done it any other way.

If I hadn't gone through what I went through, I wouldn't be the person I am today."

I'm not saying that the process is always cheery and fun—not at all. What I am saying is that we're not fortune-tellers. We can only trust that we are learning and that this learning will lead to a better place, a place where we can draw constructively from our past for new experiences we will face.

We are all familiar with the cliché "Time heals all wounds." That may be true, but often with wounds come scars. What's important is whether the scars create resentment and bitterness or lead to reflection and wisdom. As Thomas Moore writes in *Care of the Soul,* "When the soul is neglected, it doesn't just go away; it appears systematically in obsessions, addictions, violence and loss of meaning."

Life is a process, and we are here to live it. It is as if we were born to live out a mission. Throughout this process come hurts, losses and hard people. We can let this process shake us up and sap our strength, or we can trust it and move forward.

This is an invitation to trust this process called life, to keep moving against apparent odds. We keep moving and keep pushing because we all have the desire to live life to its fullest.

But there's an undertow to this desire. Witness the traumatic experiences of some of the people featured in this section. Before adults can be fully aware of their feelings, they must have internalized benevolent parental figures. If this did not occur, their need to control will act as a guard. This guard inhibits their full range of feelings and experiences. That which remains is depression, inner emptiness and inhibition. They may be reaching for the stars, but gravity keeps pulling them back to earth.

The journeys taken by those in this section address this pull of opposites. These people learn how to reconcile the drive to live life fully with a survival need to never let anyone get close, to never again risk hurt. Trusting the process is not easy.

Ultimately, we are alone, and it is up to us to answer the question, Where do I go from here? Fortunately, the answer exists within, and each person has the ability to change and grow. We are born with this.

Listen to the stories of those who have faith in a process that can heal and strengthen. Instead of becoming bitter and hardened to life, they capture the spontaneity and wisdom that is always there inside—waiting to blossom.

The stories and author reflections in this section are about people who learn to trust the process. A few of them were brought in kicking and screaming, but they did make it. What they learned is that anger is an integral part of their process. It is a necessary element that serves a purpose. That purpose is to arouse them out of their denial and lethargy, and move them toward decision and action.

Children who grow up in homes where there is neglect or any form of abuse often develop certain developmental themes. These developmental themes include difficulties with authority, problems with sexuality or issues regarding abandonment. For example, if a young man is physically abused by his father, it is quite likely that he will grow up to have problems with male authority figures in his life. This individual may have difficulties with therapists, supervisors or police officers who are male.

Years ago, a twenty-nine-year-old woman named Peggy punched a young man in the nose in a movie theater for trying to hold her hand. Peggy had been abused by her older brother. When the man, a coworker, touched her, it triggered anger and fear in Peggy, and she reacted instantly.

Many people have a fear of being abandoned. This fear can cause impulsive acting out and can lead to further estrangement and dysfunction in a relationship.

When old themes from childhood are triggered by current life events (issues with authority, abandonment, etc.), a mixture of anger and fear often surfaces. These feelings can be internalized or externalized. Examples of internalizing anger are depression, suicide and other self-destructive behaviors. Examples of externalized anger are fights and angry arguments or outbursts.

Some people are introverted—they look inside themselves for answers. Others are extroverted—they look outside themselves to find solutions to life's problems. "Richard's Story" is about a man who looked outside himself for answers. He looked to religion, and religion let him down. He describes God as a sniper. He looked to drugs for solutions. Although alcohol worked for a while, it eventually took him to the gates of hell. Richard also looked to other people for the answers. He lived for everyone else. He did what everybody else said to do. He acted the way he was supposed to. In his eyes, religion, drugs and people let him down. He took no responsibility for his problems. He became angry and raged against the institutions. He blamed his family. His parents were divorced after thirty years of marriage, and it stunned him. He blamed religion.

As you read the story, you see that Richard is not looking for the God of his parents or the emotionally crippling God of the church. He blames these Gods for creating a world he cannot relate to. Richard also blames society for his problems. He says that at times he is ready to write the human race off as irredeemable. He wonders why God created such a world. He doesn't understand how God could create sickness and war and hatred. Richard struggles with a sense of emptiness and isolation. He says he feels most of his life has been a waste and that he has in no way fulfilled his potential. Out of this emptiness and unfulfilled potential comes an incredible rage. In order to cope with his anger, Richard uses two strategies. The first is to create a world that he feels is worth living in. This fantasy world is a safe place in which Richard can express his creativity. It is much easier for Richard to be a creative genius in this fantasy world than to take a chance in the real world. Richard also uses projection as a defense against emptiness and isolation. He projects emptiness and depression out to the world. This depression then appears as paranoia. At times, Richard feels as if the world is out to get him. He thinks about giving up, going back to drinking and numbing things again, just as before.

How did Richard attempt to diminish the impact of twenty years of drinking? What did he do to soothe his anger? In the book *Care of the Soul,* Thomas Moore describes this process of healing the soul as deceptively simple. He writes, "You take back what has been disowned. You work with what is, rather than with what you wish were there." In Richard's case, he takes ownership of his anger and insecurity. Through years of therapy and a willingness to confront his past, Richard has taken control of his life. He is no longer a puppet or a victim. Richard's soul now seems open to receiving a God that will allow him to live and love and breathe. Or better stated, as Richard has learned to live and love and breathe, he has allowed God to enter his soul.

Richard is a troubled man of great depth. He has marvelous creativity that commands attention. Richard starts to understand his anger in a different way. He starts to see it as a part of his search for a spiritual home. He understands that the only way to reach home is a hard way. For so many people like

Richard, the initial steps are in the wrong direction, going backward instead of forward. That yearning is still there, however. Anger never solves a problem for Richard or brings him peace; he understands this now. He grows to understand that the one person his anger hurts the most is himself.

In addition to drugs and alcohol, Richard escapes through a system of rigid religious procedures and protocol he learned in childhood. After a while, neither of these escapes works. He begins to break these patterns by attending support meetings and learning it is all right to think for himself, free of guilt and shame, and to find his own spiritual direction. He is also able to view his family in a new light as well, even though their beliefs are not his own anymore. After years of recovery, and even more years of blaming his family for his problems and anger, he slowly reaches a point of acceptance—an acceptance that allows him to communicate more openly with them and comfortably understand that though their ways are not his, his love for them is not diminished or altered.

In *Anonymity: The Secret Life of An American Family,* Susan Bergman describes a dysfunctional family. She writes:

> If the family is where we first learn about ourselves and others, it is also often the cradle of misidentity and isolation. Our false fronts, the insecure roles we adopt to survive, the ways the "victims" of loss endure and recover, combined with our interpretations (affecting both the images that appear to us and how we ourselves are perceived), the early influences that give shape to sexuality—these are the shards that each of us sorts and reassembles, finally, must pour lives from.

In "John W.'s Story," John's life is poured into a mold. As described above, John's anger comes from his past. Things that led to anger, depression and anxiety were not dealt with or could not be dealt with, because they occurred at such an early age.

John grew up in a migrant-worker family full of explosive violence. His father physically abused his mother and John. His father also lied to John to lure him out of the house while the father planned his escape from the family. This was not the cruelest lie of all; the cruelest lie was John's father telling John that he was the reason he left.

A young child is egocentric; the world revolves around him. John believed the breakup of the family was his fault. He internalized his father's lies. Subsequently, he believed that anything negative that happened in his life was his fault.

John suffered other forms of abuse as well. He was sexually abused by his cousin and others. All of this physical and sexual abuse was multigenerational. John, now an older man and a father of nine, can only guess at what being a father is all about. He can only attempt to break long-standing family traditions of rage and abuse.

John needed to solve many problems in his life. Early on, he started drinking alcohol. For a while, it seemed to work. But there were issues of life John could not work through with alcohol. How does he learn how to parent? How does he learn how to be a husband? How does he solve problems as an adult in the world he must live in? In John's case, there was a saving grace. There were surrogates in his life. A football coach and his Uncle Lou served this role for him. They taught him about life and how best to live it. John has also gone through a recovery program for his alcoholism. This program has taught him a spiritual way of relating to the world. Finally, John has an opportunity to make amends to his children. He explores the anger and rage of his life but acknowledges the wonderful opportunity that he now has as a father—the opportunity to break the multigenerational cycle of abuse.

John W., through much heartache, anger and pain, continues to sort through the trial and the shame of his early years with his family. And while there has been much sorrow on his journey, he has continually kept his trust intact. His story, his acceptance of personal responsibility for his actions that have hurt others and his willingness to use what has happened to him in order to reach out to others no matter where he was in the process are a great lesson in faith.

In the essay "Losing a Child," the author acknowledges that even a number of years after an event, all he can do is trust and barely begin to acknowledge the truth of what every parent fears most. It's an honest and moving account.

Finally, Bill's reflection, "Digging Deep," addresses the fear many of us have about the process of recovery and its possible outcome, and how we so often spend our time trying to cut the process short.

But then again, what we eventually learn by our attempts to cut the process short is, after all, just part of the process, isn't it? It seems to be a pattern in this section, doesn't it? It was only by breaking the cycle of blame and guilt over past behaviors that these individuals were able to move on and grow beyond anger.

No one in this section has arrived. They've all been humbled in one way or another and admit that they still have a long way to go. They keep the past fresh in their minds and have no desire to go back again. But if by some chance they should, they now have the tools and the courage to break in, disrupt the process, and begin the road back.

THE PATH

You do see the path. Whether it is through tears or through joy, you see it. It calls you and asks you over and over again to put aside those things that hurt and block and wound you.

I'm scarred with the wounds of a battle, a little stooped over, a body withered by the wind and sun. Any knowledge or wisdom I have comes because of the scars and wounds. It comes from many failures and false steps.

So do not burden yourself with anger or try to walk the ungodly path of perfection. You will never make it. Your best lessons in life will not come from your great successes; they will come from making your mistakes and moving forward.

Cultivate the freshness of a child and the wisdom of an old man. Be young enough to gaze in wonder. Be wise enough to know that true beauty is stored in the heart.

—BILL CHICKERING

LOSING A CHILD

On a recent flight to Columbus, Ohio, I sat next to a mother nursing her newborn daughter. Her son sat in the seat beside her. It made me remember.

In my family there were two children. My younger sister and I were three years apart in age. I grew up with this model of a family.

As my wife and I started our family, we had a son. As he approached age three, my wife became pregnant again. The test revealed that it was a little girl. My son would now have a younger sister. As far as I was concerned, this would make the family complete.

The pregnancy progressed smoothly until the third trimester. As the ninth month arrived, my wife knew there was a problem. I guess when you're that close, you just know. I tried to stay calm while the doctors monitored her closely.

Late one afternoon, my wife called and told me to meet her at the hospital. With great apprehension, I hurried to Arnold Palmer Children's Hospital. When I arrived, she told me that our little girl was dead.

I wanted to be angry, but instead, I just shut down emotionally. It was so unfair. You do the right thing, try to be a good person and this happens. My wife still had to go through the pain of delivering the child.

She delivered a perfectly formed little girl, but something went terribly wrong. The doctors said it was a virus. Our little girl would never know her big brother. He would never be able to play with her. We would never have the chance to watch her grow.

At 1:00 A.M. I left the hospital and my wife to go home. I had done what I know how to do—take charge. I made all the arrangements with the hospital and the funeral home. I tried to take care of my wife. I made phone calls to the family. And when I got home, I stared at the wall. There was no one anywhere to get angry at. There was no one to explain why.

For the first time, my anger began to well up from deep inside. Without a target and a place to dissipate, it led me into a state of depression. For me it was a cold and lonely place to stay until I reached the other side.

All my life I have wanted to control my environment and make things all right. But I couldn't control this. I couldn't control the level of depression experienced by my wife or my alternating depression, anger and psychic numbness.

For many years, I had worked professionally with families going through incredible loss and grief. Colleagues and teachers spoke of the magic of the grief process. I had observed the process in many people. I knew it took time—sometimes it took years.

But it had never really happened to my wife and me before. This first-hand experience taught me about the differences between the male and female grieving processes. It just seemed my wife and I could not get on the same page. When she wanted to be hugged, I was generally shut down. I have much more empathy for others today.

Looking back, five years later, I still don't understand. I know things happen, but I don't know why this happened. I still don't know the reason. The doctors said it was a virus. But why? I understand that bad things happen to good people and that the good people are not at fault. Wounds can eventually heal with good friends and sufficient time.

And you can't begin to grasp what happened until you begin to look back at it years later.

It's all a test of faith, I suppose.

Stand Back

What do you see in her broken heart? You wonder how
Much more ego beating she can stand before she folds.

It is not fair, it is not right. Do not throw your anger at the
wrong people; I do tell you that they suffer enough already.

What you seek will come through a quiet and calm seeking
of the Spirit; it will not come through harshness and venom.

Let your words be the burning ones of the Spirit; let your
words be the knives that cut through to the truth. Stand
your ground; disrespect no one, neither accept disrespect
from anyone.

Do not quarrel or punish yourself for your words tonight. I,
perhaps more than anyone, will tell you that anger is a very
appropriate and necessary response to an injustice.

But stand back now; the truth, clearly spoken, is always your best
weapon. Calmly spoken, it can burn a hole through the hardest
heart.

—BILL CHICKERING

Live-In

The anger gets lost in the night;
It pushes too hard.
Live in a mood of expectancy, for you
will not be left alone;
nor your talents untouched;
nor your words unwritten—

You will always have these; even
on nights when you and the anger
believe you're alone;
call up words of hope and sing some
new songs—

Deliver peace with the conviction of love.
Live in peace, and find your way down a new set
of tracks.

—BILL CHICKERING

RICHARD'S STORY

When I was told this was going to be a book about anger, I laughed. Boy, if they wanted to talk about anger, they sure came to the right person. Sometimes I think I've got enough anger in me to loan out to a few other people. When it's not right up front, it's usually low-grade and simmering in the background. Even sitting down and trying to write this is getting me upset. I don't know whether I'll have the words, and I don't know where to start.

I feel that most of my life has been a waste. Not that I haven't learned a lot; it's just that I know how much potential I've always had and how little I've used.

Since this is about anger—I'm angry that I threw twenty years of my life away to alcohol and living like there was no tomorrow. The only reason I halfway believe that there's a God is that there is little reason I should be alive today, except that someone else has got something in mind for me. The amounts I drank should have killed me. This one photograph still haunts me. It was taken about two months before I quit. I'm at my parent's home on vacation. I'm sitting in a chair looking pretty relaxed. I'm holding a tumbler full of whiskey, with the rest of the bottle on the table beside me. My body looks bloated, and my face has red patches all over it. I still cringe whenever I look at it.

I began drinking when I was a teenager and continued to the point where I was drinking nearly a fifth of whiskey a day when I quit. My last few days drinking were spent in my apartment with the doors locked, the windows shut and the blinds pulled tight. I drank, took showers to sober up, ate a little bit of food, screamed at God, cried and punched holes through the walls. I had never, ever known what it was like to be at what they called "the bottom." But I was there.

The longer I stayed away from alcohol, the more my feelings came back—feelings of intense joy, hurt, pain, sexual feelings and depression, to name just a few.

I didn't want to get near the feelings—didn't want to even get close. Some good friends told me this was normal. I had buried my emotions and feelings behind alcohol for so long that when they started to come up while I was sober, I panicked. I was in brand-new territory. I had nowhere to run this time.

And all this alcohol, this addiction, all this anger—what is it? I believe it's part of my search for a spiritual home—a place where I can rest in the arms of God and know I am where I belong. Author M. Scott Peck said it well when he wrote, "The only way to reach home is the hard way. But addicts, who have a terrible powerful yearning to go home, are going the wrong way—back instead of forward . . . in this yearning to go home, addicts are people who have a more powerful calling than most to the spirit, to God, but they simply have the directions of the journey mixed up."

I am angry at what I've filled my life with. And, most of all, I am angry at those who told me that I had to find redemption, their kind of redemption: a kind religiosity and piousness that were not the answer for me then and are not now. It was the kind of path that cut me off from the Spirit, a path that did not change until I walked away from the well-dressed Sundays of a church life that bored me. My path changed even more when I held the hand of an alcoholic, crack addict or heroin addict around a table in a small room—bowing my head and saying the Lord's Prayer with them.

It has been harder to break the bonds of that religious training than it ever was to stop drinking. Every time I see a religious tract or run across a television preacher, a streak of pure hatred runs through me. This isn't getting me anywhere either, and won't until I let go of the hate, let them live as they live and leave them alone.

But the anger is still there, and will not leave until I'm done with it—not a moment sooner. I think of all those years, stuffing myself in one pew after another, in one church after another, in one denomination after another, thinking that maybe this would be the time when I "got it," that this would be the time when their message would get through.

But it never did.

Even now, as I write this, there is the sense that I'm not getting it out the way I want. I sit here, a middle-aged man who has spent his life doing what everyone told him to do and living the way everyone told him to live. I was taught that was the way to do things—that was the way to get by—because, after all, the most important thing in life is to make sure that everyone else likes you and make sure everyone approves of what you're doing. You may feel like a train wreck, but that's not important. What is important is that everyone around you thinks that you're a "fine young man."

From the time I was a child, the most important thing to me was to get away by myself and be alone. At least for a few minutes each day I could have some thoughts and some dreams that were all mine. I buried my thoughts in books and in the stories I made up in my head. In those stories, I could be who I wanted to be. I listened to my own voice and did what I wanted to do.

Even today I do the same things: I dream of heroics and conquests, of following my own path, succeeding, and laughing at the people and the God of my past.

And who was the God of my past? I recall a therapist posing a very odd question right in the middle of a session. He stopped what he was saying and suddenly asked, "What do you picture when you picture God?"

Even though the question was sudden, my answer came quickly. "God," I said, "is a sniper. He sits hidden in a tree with a high-powered gun, just waiting for me to make a mistake. As soon as I do, he nails me."

I still think of God that way from time to time.

I am looking for God, not for the God of my parents, or the God of my family, or the emotionally crippling God of the church. I am looking for a God that allows his people to live and love, and breathe and create, and fail and get on with it.

I am angry for all of the poetry I've never written because I was afraid. I am angry at all the angry words I've never written to God because I was taught that was not right. I was even told by someone, "I hope you're not angry at God." I am full of rage at the verse and language that has never appeared, beautiful verse that stuck in my throat until I swallowed.

Just where do I turn my rage? Where does it go? The safest place is right here on these pages, I guess. No one will get hurt, and I can hit the keys as hard as I want. "You can't be angry at God." Like hell, you can't. I have read the psalms of King David in the Bible. That was one angry man who spent a lot of time getting very angry with God.

I am ashamed of all I have not done in this life. I feel cheated when I think how much has passed me by and how much I've missed because I didn't want to get someone pissed off or because I wanted to please someone who couldn't have cared less.

Today I am a very angry man, mad at all those things you're not supposed to be angry at. And I want to find my way home—on my terms this time, speaking to God the way I want. The churches I left would be better off sold and the money given to the poor. At least that way someone would benefit and we wouldn't have so many amateur theologians running around telling us what to believe, how to believe it and who to vote for. It is a world I want no part of.

What I do know is that I lived in a world of denial until I was in my mid-twenties. For years, I recall thinking we had a great family, that nothing ever went wrong in our family and that we would always be together. Stuff went bad only in other families—not ours.

Then came the day my mother told me that she and Dad were getting a divorce after thirty years of marriage. I was stunned. Mom recounted a litany of things that had gone on over the years. They were things I was totally unaware of. I didn't have a clue, no knowledge at all. I guess that shows how deeply my family hid things. From time to time, I think back and remember things that should have warned me that everything was not all right. But fantasy has a very strong pull on us, and we believe what we want to believe.

What will I find when I burrow down deep into my spirit? What will I unearth? When you hit the first level, you'll throw out a shovel full of discomfort, somewhat irritating, but nothing that can't be fixed with a nice hour-long massage.

When you hit the deepest level, you'll come to a door; I'll come to a door. I do not know what lies there, what is waiting. My feeling right now is that it is more anger than I've dreamed possible: everything I never did, every word I never wrote, every kind thought I never acted upon, every opportunity I ever lost. It's probably a swirling, jumbled mess with no focus and no message.

I often go numb when the chance to feel something gets too close, when an actual emotion gets too near to me. I feel the fear when I hear a kind voice, a compliment or a positive remark about my appearance or my work.

And I remember with utter disbelief the drivel taught to me about God. And I saw it again today in the letter a friend sent me. It was quite odd, actually. A three-page, single-spaced letter. He had just been let go from a missionary organization because he couldn't raise enough money to keep himself working. That's right. He was working for an organization that made him raise contributions for his own salary. My God, I wish I were kidding about that, but I'm not.

My friend's a great guy; don't get me wrong. It's just that I felt more and more pain and more and more anger the longer I read. I cringed as he tried to quickly explain away emotions and feelings in jargon. And as he described some trouble he'd been having, it seems that an untrained counselor managed to solve it and put it to rest in two sessions! Two sessions! I've been seeing a therapist for three years, and I'm just starting to get near some reality, just beginning to feel all the nerve endings wake up. I hope things go well for my friend. I'm going to stay in touch and see what's going on. The letter brought back all my fear again. Because I remember when I was using the language my friend uses now, and I remember all the tears and anger that have exploded from me since those days. I'm glad I didn't know how far I had to go.

I would guess that I'm about ten years out of that religious prison. Just barely starting to get comfortable, barely away from all the guilt and away from the gut feeling that told me I wasn't good enough for God's love, I still hadn't proven enough yet and in God's eyes, I would never quite earn my keep. There are days when I still look over my shoulder, still judge my every thought and action to see whether I've done it correctly.

There are a lot of days when I want to quit—just go back to drinking and start numbing things all over again.

I get very angry about my problems with sexuality. I still feel like a little kid who never got answers to some very basic questions about sex. I just don't think our family even talked about it. And that's cost me as well. It has helped to keep the fear rolling around inside me. I feel naïve and guilty. Sex is still the most fearful area for a lot of people, and for me. I don't feel comfortable with my sexuality. It makes me very nervous sometimes.

And why keep writing? Because it's helping me get a lot of garbage out in the open. It's helping me to take a few minutes to try to understand why I seem to be on edge a lot and why I seem to run from the happiness and success that comes my way. I could sit here and blame a lot of people, assign responsibility. But that never seems to get me anywhere either.

The deeper I get into this story, the more I find that anger seems to be a part of me, seems to be simmering somewhere most of the time. So, how does that anger come out? Does it stay in? Just what do I do with it?

A lot of anger simply stays inside me. It never makes it outside. It boils up as depression, headaches, neck pain, heart palpitations and a burning stomach. For the last three months, I've been putting myself through a pretty rigorous workout program—the weights, the aerobics, the stretching exercises, the whole thing. And I guess I could say that it's working. More of my anger gets out these days, whether it's through exercise or by not holding back when I feel really upset or by simply stating my mind when I disagree with something.

I'm under no illusion that all the anger I have inside will simply fade away or that someday I'll find out what it's all about. I really don't think I will. What's going on these days in my therapy sessions is pretty amazing. I'll start talking about something that once hurt me, that I dusted off and said didn't matter when it really did. The tears start to come, but so does the anger. Sometimes I just don't think I realize how much I've locked away.

My opinion of people in general has veered wildly over the years. One day I'll be amazed at how kind and generous people can be and how genuinely caring. The next day I'll be ready to write off the human race as irredeemable. I'm a voracious reader. I'll read about all the sickness, strife, war, hatred and inhumanity and wonder why God lets it go on another minute, why life seems to be one long process of digging yourself out from under one problem or another. If you're a celebrity, that's good, because you can make a lot of money publishing books about your breakdowns and miscues. If you're not, well, just suffer alone.

The problem is that I keep getting upset about how other people behave, which is something I ought not concern myself with because I really don't have any control over it. Yet somehow I still convince myself occasionally that if I could just change a few things in several people, life would be fine—just fine.

It seems, however, that people don't want to cooperate in my rehabilitation efforts on their behalf. And so I remain angry.

Where all that anger really surfaced was within my family. We parted company over a number of issues years ago. So each visit, every two years or so, was an adventure. And the last visit was no exception. It seems as though we communicate to each other through interpreters. My brother will tell me how Dad feels about something I did. I'll tell my sister how I react to Mom's behavior. My sister will tell me about my brother, my brother about my sister, and I'll talk to either one of them about the other. What happens is this: No one knows about how anyone is really feeling about anything because no one talks directly with the person they need to deal with. We all punctuate our remarks with, "Now don't tell (Mom, Dad, brother, sister) what I just said. They might really get upset."

Will that method of communication ever change? Actually, the answer is yes. Over the past couple of years, after going through several severe crises, we're talking again. It's a gift I never thought would show up. But it has, and I'm very grateful. And we're talking to one another about things that matter, not just the weather or politics (they still have a long way to go in that area!).

Though I'm still angry at what went on in our family when I was young, I find that tolerance and forgiveness have begun to creep into my conversation. Sometimes I even try to stop them when they come because, after all, being pissed is so much more fun.

I guess this is as good a spot as any to go back to where I started. I believe more and more every day that what I'm looking for is something spiritual, not something that can be touched or handled, but a path that brings some measure of peace through all the bumps, bruises, heartache and joy. There is a Zen saying that touches on all of this: "Before enlightenment—chop wood, carry water. After enlightenment—chop wood, carry water." What that means to me is that while my life, my routine, may not change much from day to day, the way I look at life will. What I discover will not come through a brilliant flash of light from the heavens, but through the lessons learned from ordinary things and ordinary people every day.

Anger is not the "way home" for me. It has never solved a problem or brought me peace, and at times it still burns hot. The one it has hurt the most is me; the spirit it's poisoned the most is mine.

I hope I've learned my lessons by now.

DIGGING DEEP

Don't trust anyone who isn't angry.

—John Trudel
Native-American musician

It's difficult to explore, to dig in, tunnel through and find out what's really going on. Very few people, if any, enjoy doing it. It requires dogged determination and a willingness to possibly discover things that we'd rather not take a look at.

And given that ours is a culture based on immediate gratification, the fact that this exploration may take some time is even more annoying. We want to find out the reasons now; we want to fix things now. Sooner than now would be fine, but we'll settle for now if that's all we can get.

Therapy and counseling can jump-start the process, but even then it's a matter of our willingness to cooperate in it. If we wish to be stubborn, we can blow a lot of money and then blame the professional when our psyche isn't repaired as quickly as we'd get over a cold or a hangnail. How much repair does the psyche need anyway?

Why is it we're so uncomfortable with substance and depth? Why do we prefer to skim the surface rather than hold our breath and plunge in? The only reason I can come up with is that we're scared. At least I know I am. I think of the times a counselor has asked me a question that has made me squirm and then started drilling the well-defended façade I'd been building for over forty-five years.

It's not that the façade is completely false; it's just not the whole story—especially the anger part of the story. That's the part I'll plow under quicker than anything. I like to be seen as together and under control—very level and even. Those are the qualities I'd like you to go home and share with others. They're the ones I'd like you to remember me by.

So for years I stayed calm and stayed cool because that's what I believed everyone wanted to see. That was my own illusion at work. What I've discovered since then is that most people prefer a much more well-rounded individual, someone less placid, with a little more passion and fire.

I stayed cool and stuffed it. If I was hurt, I never told anyone; if someone offended me, I kept quiet and went along with it. In a lively discussion, I'd agree with everyone, even people with divergent points of view. Most of the time if I saw an injustice, I'd let it go. If I was overworked and tired and yet was asked to do still one more thing, I'd take it on and when I burned out, blame the person who made the request.

I was well liked for the most part—and absolutely miserable. You couldn't really say I had a faith of any sort. What I had embraced to keep the wolves at bay was a system with a lot of unwritten rules and unwritten consequences: when you could think, what you could think and what you could think about it. You didn't have to think, actually. All the answers were prepared for you in advance.

Psychologist Robert Johnson, in *Owning Your Own Shadow*, writes, "The religious process consists of restoring the wholeness of the personality. The word religion means to re-late, to put back together again, to heal the wounds of separation."

And that's what I was—separated and cut off. I had a religion of the heart that wanted desperately to believe in a God of forgiveness, a God who accepted me—warts and all. But I lived in a religion of the culture and the workplace—a religion that forgave little, expected a lot and usually shot its wounded to thin the herd.

And so I'm learning—still learning. It's amazing how long it took me to take a look inside. I've listened to all the promises of all the quick-fix gurus that clog the bookstores and all the hucksters on the infomercials. In fact, I've actually bought a few of the products advertised: books, tapes, inspirational music and CDs. What I've gained from all that is a large credit card bill and a lot of stuff gathering in a closet and living in well-deserved darkness. The dream the charlatans sell is also peculiarly American in that it promises to satisfy our need for instant gratification and satisfaction. The big lie we're sold is this: "At some point in time, sooner rather than later, you will be fixed. What was bothering you will be done. You can live at the peak all the time."

It's sad that millions of people are buying this. They've been led to believe that they can live permanently on the mountaintop, that if they don't, something they're doing is wrong or they need to learn a system a little more thoroughly. Then they'll have it right.

But learning stops at the peak. Why? Because you can climb no higher, go no further. Our lives are not defined by the peaks; they're defined by what we learn in the valleys and what we come to understand when the climb begins to get steep.

It has taken me a long time to understand this, a long time to even start to learn the religion of the heart and discover a God of my understanding who accepts me as whole, with all my good points, bad points, compassion, egotism and selflessness. I know that I am both deeply gifted and deeply flawed, both light and shadow. For many years, I lived on the surface, knowing all the time what was beneath me and ignoring it, trying to banish anger, frustration, fear and imperfection—especially imperfection.

I am many sided, multifaceted, often right and often wrong, often angry and often joyous—both saint and sinner.

And I can live with that.

JOHN W.'S STORY

In many ways I'm still overwhelmed by my anger. Even after thirteen years of sobriety and a lot of hard work, I still feel that I have a long way to go. There are still things in my past that I have obviously not dealt with and are still so painful that right now I can only pray for them to be relieved.

It is difficult to deal with anger when my first memory, at

about age three or four, is that of my mother crouched behind the couch with blood streaming down her face. I can hear her screaming at my father and see my father with his fists clenched tight. I don't know if those images will ever leave me.

I remember a lot of incidents, but I'll talk about a few in particular. One evening I was in my bed, sound asleep. My father came in unannounced and gave me a hard spanking. To this day I do not know why.

On another occasion, my mother and sister and I went to an island off Puget Sound to pick berries. I was excited because I knew that when I got home, I was going to get to spend the weekend with my father. While we were out, he was at home fixing up the house (I realize now it was because he was getting ready to leave us). I got on a passenger boat to take me to the dock, where we had agreed to meet. I kept waiting until I resigned myself to the fact that he was not going to show up. I gave up and finally hitchhiked my way home. I was eight or nine years old at the time. It turned out he had stayed at home and continued to work on the house. He didn't mention anything about not meeting me at the dock. He told me to play and later on sent me to the store on an errand. While I was at the store, I used a penny I had to buy some candy. When I got back home, he saw the candy and told me what a bad person I'd been for stealing it. He said he was leaving us. When I started to cry, he said, "That's what you get for being a thief."

I felt sorry for my father later in my life because I realized he was an alcoholic and came from an abusive home himself. That still doesn't excuse what he did, but I was glad that my years in recovery from addiction had given me some compassion for him.

There were other scenes with my father that still make me feel angry and sorrowful. Once, after an absence of several years, he approached me after I'd played a hard football game, put his arms around me, and gave me a hug. I remember how embarrassed I felt.

In 1950 I got married. On my wedding day the church was full, and my brother and I were waiting behind the altar. The attendants put down a white runner on which the bride would walk. The first person down it was my dad. He walked to the front pew, shoved my mother aside and sat down. I had to physically restrain my brother from attacking him. He sat there through the wedding, and when my new wife and I turned around to face the congregation, he was gone.

I didn't see him for another ten months. Then, the day of my first child's baptism, he showed up at our home with a roast and invited himself in for dinner. When I told him we were going to the baptism, he said, "I thought it would be something like that." He left, and I never saw him again, even though he lived to be ninety years old. One of the reasons I still harbor anger toward him is that he was never repentant for anything that he did. And the fact that he had a rough childhood does not make it right.

I have nine children myself—six boys and three girls. In 1995, at the age of thirty-four, one of my sons killed himself in a Las Vegas hotel room. He was an addict, and he could not cope. He left a note that said he was totally burned out. The note also said, "If you need anything, call my dad." Even though I'm angry at the way my son died, I do take some comfort in the fact that he did mention me in the note.

I had to guess at how to be a father, and since my own recovery from addiction, my kids have told me that I was a good dad. But my alcoholism was not without its consequences; I am still estranged from one son who lives out West.

At times it's impossible for me to completely let go of the anger and the past. There are two parts of my life that anger me the most and still cause me pain. One is the sexual abuse I suffered, and the other is my disease of alcoholism. I was sexually abused between the ages of seven and nine by my cousin. He touched me and made me touch him. And as is often the case with sexual abuse, there was a thrill but no real enjoyment. There was just a lot of shame. I was also sexually abused by a neighbor and by others.

But the time that is burned into my memory was once when my cousin abused me on the farm. I told my sister what had happened and made sure to tell her not to tell my mom. Well, she did. My mom's response was, "Don't be silly. Your cousin wouldn't do that." Talk about feeling like nothing.

The incongruity in my story is that I remember being basically a happy child. I grew up during the Depression, and my family was very poor, even though I didn't know it at the time. Our family made a living as migrant workers. My mother was the one who held the family together; I rarely remember my father being at home.

I did have some good influences. One was my football coach. He was like a surrogate father to me, and he encouraged me and helped me stay in school. The other was my uncle Lou. When I went fishing, I would bring my catch back to him. He would praise me for what I had done, and then we cooked and ate my catch. He was always telling me what a good fisherman I was. I made sure I used Uncle Lou as a model for the way I treated my own children.

But even though I had surrogate fathers, I did not know much of anything about money or family life. Those two basics eluded me for a long time.

So there have been a lot of losses in my life, losses that have caused me a lot of hurt and anger and shame, especially the shame from the abuse, both emotional and physical. That lasts to this day.

Another loss was my marriage. I would tell God I felt betrayed by him for allowing me to go into a marriage that was so dysfunctional right from the beginning. I have only really disliked two people in my life, and one of them was my ex-wife; I had a lot of anger and resentment toward her. When I got into a recovery program, I realized I needed to let go of the resentments and the anger. I also learned that I had no right to abuse women emotionally and sexually just because of the anger I harbored toward my marriage and toward my ex-wife.

Needless to say, all the problems I had in my life were exacerbated by my alcoholism. I drank from 1949 until I sobered up in 1983. Toward the end of my marriage, I began to isolate myself and have blackouts. I lost patients in my dental practice because I had a habit of sleeping on the floor of my office. At one point, I felt so low that I had to reach up just to touch the bottom.

At my first AA meeting, I practically screamed, "Thank God I'm an alcoholic!" I was glad a friend told me what my problem was, because I thought I was just angry, crazy and scared. Because of my recovery, I was able to handle the death of my son and begin to make some amends to my children for my behavior while I was drinking.

One of my favorite phrases is from the movie *A Long Hot Summer*. At one point the father says to Angela Lansbury, "I feel so good I think I'll live forever." Well, I may not live forever, but I can sure live with that feeling. I have seen a lot of negative situations in my life, but I know today that there is hope. I know that we all can make it.

I remember listening to a recovery tape. The speaker talked about his mom and dad, and how even though he thinks they did a lousy job at times, he now realizes that they did the best that they could with what they had. That is a good and forgiving attitude to have because it places the responsibility on ourselves for how we turn out. I know I made mistakes as a father, but I also know that I did the best that I could. Today, I believe that the best way I can overcome the anger, resentments and mistakes of the past is by making amends to my children. Hopefully, my kids will make amends to their children as well, and we can keep this cycle going in our family. And finally, through succeeding generations, we can achieve just what we were put on this earth to be.

ISLAND HOPPING

As you can see from the stories in this book, getting over anger is a process. Some do it quickly, and others take more time. I have no patience with the abstract sermonizers who say, "Just get over it. Let it go." My response is usually, "Shut up. It's my anger. I want to let it go, but it's decided it doesn't want to leave right now. I'm going to talk to some people about it, and you're sure not one of them."

We all need to talk about it.

We're a complicated lot, we human beings. There are times when we'll get angrier about big things than about little things, and there are times when we'll let go of the big things quicker than the little things. That's just the way we are. And those who preach simplicity leave me cold. Yes, I know unresolved anger will only hurt me, and yes, I know I have to let things go. But even the Old Testament says God was angry with his chosen people for centuries. So cut me a little slack. Let me chat with some folks, and I'll be fine.

Those folks are my islands, people who are "edged with sand." They've got their problems, just as I have, but they still have room to let me in.

When the anger's caving in on me, I start floating between these islands, making a brief stop at each one. At some, I have a quick conversation; at others, I just check in; and at some of the stops, I unpack my bags and stay awhile. I'm usually pretty good at knowing when it's time to go.

Anger and isolation: They're just like oil and water—they don't mix. They can't touch each other. I know about isolation because I've tried it. I create demons out of nothing and lions out of pussycats—making up imaginary conversations and scenarios in which I usually end up standing in conquest over my fallen prey. When I make it up, I never lose. I've acted out a few of those fantasies, before talking with anyone, and without exception they've ended in disaster.

So I drift between my islands. I call, stop in or drop a note in a bottle. And most people, it seems, have enough room to let me stand.

Lessons

INTRODUCTION

Are most of the problems we face really as large as we make them out to be? Do we often give others power over our lives? Do we perceive life's events through a catastrophic set of glasses? You've heard it before: It's all in the eyes of the beholder. This chapter contains stories about loss and about learning. These stories illustrate the loss of power and the ultimate finding of one's power. As attorney Gerry Spence says in the book *How to Argue and Win Every Time,* "If I have endowed the other with power that the other does not possess, then I face my own power, do I not? My own power has become my opponent, my enemy."

The people in these stories strive to regain a sense of power. The lessons they learn are existential ones.

The lesson is captured in "Steps" in the words

> Roses will bloom,
> The skies will rain and snow . . .
> And it will all happen whether you
> Lock up inside, or whether
> You let it go.

The individuals in these stories have an understanding of the world that causes them pain and anger. They try desperately to relieve these emotions. They feel powerless. They are alone, but out of this aloneness comes their acceptance.

They find only one road to take. This road leads them back to themselves. These people take a fearless look at their own existence. Instead of remaining in rigid, "locked," self-defeating patterns, they change. First, by letting it all go. Second, by accepting their existence. Third, by reclaiming their own power.

As they travel the road of life, they learn some lessons. Anger plays an integral part in these lessons. Sometimes the anger is appropriate, and often it is misdirected. One thing is for sure: It is much easier to judge when the anger can be evaluated from a distance.

When you come right down to it, we all have to stand alone. At least that's the existential perspective. Sartre wrote that existence precedes essence. What our lives are like and how we live them determines the core—our essence. By changing the patterns of our lives, it is possible to exchange a painful core for one that is less painful or one that is even optimistic. By accepting their life as it really is, the people in these stories begin to live in the moment. Their minds are open to all potential, and they learn to drink of the present. As Phil

Jackson, the head coach of the Chicago Bulls, writes in his book, *Sacred Hoops:*

> What pollutes the mind in the Buddhist view is our desire to get life to conform to our particular notion of how things should be, as opposed to how they really are. In the course of everyday life, we spend the majority of our time immersed in self-centered thoughts. Why did this happen to me? What would make me feel better? If only I could make more money, win her heart, make my boss appreciate me. The thoughts themselves are not the problem; it's our desperate clinging to them and our resistance to what is actually happening that causes us so much anguish.

The first chapter of this section is "Lost and Found." In it the contributors talk about recovering a part of themselves that they loved, but had somehow misplaced along the way. John T. shared with us the recovery of his strength and personal faith after the death of his closest friend. Deborah wrote of recovering the soft and compassionate side of her personality that she had buried for many years under a blanket of bitterness and anger.

In the second chapter, "Trusting the Process," were the words of courageous people who broke through destructive behaviors and patterns, and replaced them with actions and attitudes that started them on a journey back to their emotional health and personal satisfaction. John W. broke through his anger, blame and guilt. Allen broke through some wishful thinking and gained self-respect by beginning to think more pragmatically and decisively.

And though we title this chapter "Lessons," it could just as easily have been called "What I Learned Through All of This."

The first story in the section is Diane's. She tells a painful story about broken bonds of trust and deceit. Those of us who have ever been damaged or abused by someone in whom we placed our faith and confidence will resonate with her story. We see how Diane uses her anger to wake up and take action. That is her lesson, and it came at quite a price.

The contributors to this final chapter all walked away with some good lessons in tow. Diane learns to stop blaming herself for being deceived. She was probably in one of the most vulnerable spots a person can be in—leaning heavily on someone for support and counsel, only to have that someone take advantage of her vulnerability. Diane was able to get beyond her shame when she embraced anger as her friend; when she did that, the misplaced responsibility for what had happened to her was placed where it belonged—back on the shoulders of the perpetrator.

What happened to Diane has often been described as repetition compulsion. It seems when an individual is hurt early in life, that hurt is often replicated throughout life. Diane was abused at age seven. The perpetrator was someone she trusted. Now here she is back in the same situation with another male authority figure, her therapist.

In Diane's family there were many rules. All of these rules were geared toward keeping secrets: Don't tell anyone about what happens in the family. As long as no one knows, the family is all right. Stuff your feelings because feelings are bad. Certainly this makes anger the worst of emotions. Don't think about what is going on, just shut down and keep it all a secret. Diane learned these lessons well.

In keeping the secrets, Diane feels helplessness. Out of this feeling comes a sense that she is trapped. These are the same feelings she had in her youth—feelings of being helpless and trapped. It is easy to understand a seven-year-old's feeling of being out of control, especially when they are being manipulated by an adult. But now that Diane is an adult, it is difficult for her and for others to understand her need for secrecy. She is in a situation that invokes ire in all those who know and care for her. They wonder why she can't deal with this openly and get it behind her. It is not that simple for Diane.

The helplessness that Diane is experiencing finally leads to frustration. This frustration produces anger. Ultimately, the anger and resulting pain bring her to action. Instead of stuffing the anger, she uses its power to motivate her to change. Maybe there is a formula here. Maybe that formula is: When the pain increases to a level where it becomes unbearable, a person will change. Maybe the gym phrase "No pain—no gain" is a metaphor for life's changes and even life's lessons.

Life is full of ups and downs. Diane has a choice. She can go with the lessons of the flow or beat her angry head against the source of her discomfort. She has faith and conviction, and makes the right choice. She uses the anger to take a stand, a stand she avoided for too long. Anger has become her friend and source of strength.

Sometimes, when we get too close, it is easy to pick up the confusion and pain of another person. Stepping away and looking at the situation from a clearer perspective allows for balance. Diane didn't isolate, but she alone made the decision to act. Talking to those she trusted helped her to do that.

Individuals who have suffered some narcissistic injury or other form of deep developmental hurt seem to possess deep-rooted anger. As mention earlier in this book, some people internalize this anger. They withdraw, become depressed or may participate in self-destructive behavior. Some people externalize this anger. They become angry, full of rage and sometimes even violent. Others deal with their anger openly. It comes out quickly, and they put it behind them. If the outburst is not destructive and there can be moments of contemplation, this way of dealing with anger can certainly be educational. Lastly, there are people like Faye. They are so overwhelmed with life's events that to let the anger out at once would shatter them completely.

There are many strategies people can employ to keep the hurt in place. These strategies help them to repress the old pain and anger. Regardless of what style individuals choose, they have to deal with the consequences. Faye faces the moment alone. Her whole world is falling down around her. Faye's story almost rivals that of Job in the Bible. How does she endure? Fay keeps going, as if to stop running would allow the overwhelming pain and anger to catch up with her. After a while, she starts to let the anger out slowly.

Faye looks at her anger only in bits and spurts. She feels that she hasn't allowed much of it out yet. Her style is to allow the anger to leak out slowly in its own time. She does this when she feels she can handle it. Her self-talk statements are much like that of a workaholic. She says, "I have to keep going. I can't stop. I have to keep producing." If she stops, there is a sense that she would be overwhelmed with the burden of an unbearable rage.

Faye closes off and shuts down. A part of her self-talk strategy involves saying that she doesn't have the right to act out her anger. Faye always thought that after all she had been through, there would be some kind of reward waiting for her, as if endurance and persistence could get her to the finish line. She entertains the notion that if she acts out her anger, it will destroy whatever reward she had coming. Her belief systems about anger are distorted and generally unproductive.

"Faye's Story" illustrates the ups and downs of a tumultuous life. She willingly acknowledges that it is a story of lessons that are still in process, and freely admits that she has a long way to go when it comes to dealing with her anger in more constructive and personally beneficial ways.

Pay special attention to other stories in this chapter. In "The Loss of a Dream," a new father projects his dreams onto his newborn son. In this story, the young child has an illness that does not allow the father's dreams to be fulfilled. Notice in the story how by paying attention the boy teaches the father everything he needs to know.

CATCH ME IF YOU CAN

I think the most elusive thing in the world is faith: the faith not to control, the faith not to panic and act in anger, the faith that keeps you from fear.

Some people seem to hold effortlessly to faith. Others grasp and struggle and sweat, and always seem to come up empty.

But maybe the problem is in the struggling. Maybe faith comes when you stop grasping. Maybe it comes at the point where you simply don't understand anymore. Maybe it's at that point that we "know" enough to finally let go.

What my own struggle with faith tells me is this: That while I believe God took care of me yesterday and today, I still doubt that God will do it again tomorrow.

That's it basically.

DIANE'S STORY

There are times when anger can be helpful, times when it can help you to make decisions and take some stands about your life that you've been avoiding for far too long. That's what my story is about.

Back in the late 1960s I went into treatment for alcoholism. I was very scared, but I was also willing to trust anyone who wanted to lend me a hand and support me while I was going through treatment. While in treatment, I met a therapist, someone I trusted, someone who helped raise my self-esteem and made me feel good about myself again. When I got out of treatment, I started seeing him on an individual basis.

That's when the sexual abuse started. I was in my mid-twenties at the time. (This is really hard to talk about.) This person was married, and that made things even worse. He abused me for a year. I was scared to death and didn't know whom to turn to. The therapist told me that this would just be a secret between us.

But I couldn't keep it a secret any longer. The whole thing was just really sick, so I told a friend of mine about what was going on. I told her how unhappy I was and that I didn't know how I was staying sober through all of this.

One day my friend called me and told me that she could no longer keep the secret. She would have to tell someone else about this. It was then that I knew I had to take some action.

So I went and talked to another friend about the abuse by this therapist. What she said next surprised me; the same therapist had also abused her, and there were a lot of people who didn't like what this guy was doing. There turned out to be many more victims of his abuse.

I felt scared and betrayed and hurt. In my confused head, I had managed to let myself think that he had actually cared about me, even though I knew for a fact that he didn't. It also brought the past screaming back at me—how I had been abused by a neighborhood man, also someone I trusted. And here I was, back in the same spot again.

But through all of this, I did not lose faith in people, and I thought enough of myself to stay away from drinking and drugging. I got a referral to another therapist and also got a very good AA sponsor, the woman I credit with saving my life.

I was honest with my new therapist, and she asked me some tough questions. She asked me what I was going to do when this guy showed up at my front door. I couldn't believe this would ever happen, but I guess she knew enough about patterns of abuse to think it might.

And it did. One day there was a knock at my front door, and it was him. To this day I cannot tell you what he said, but I never let him in the house. I thank my anger for giving me the strength to turn him away and say enough is enough.

While working with a new therapist, I discovered that I really had some issues with men, and I've been working hard on these. One of the first things I decided was that I would never see a male therapist again. And I've also learned to trust other women a lot more.

As to the therapist that abused others and me, I was told by one professional to turn him in. But I thought no one would believe me; he had been turned in before, and nothing had happened.

Today I am in a much better place, both emotionally and relationally. In fact, I've been able to help others who went through experiences similar to mine, and I feel very good about that.

I think back to that time nearly thirty years ago. I think about how exciting it was to keep secrets. Today, however, I do my very best not to keep secrets. It's just too unhealthy for me to play that game anymore.

I met my husband about two years after that ordeal, and we've been married nearly twenty-five years. We have a very healthy and happy relationship.

But there are still times when I remember the past and punish myself for it. When I was abused at the age of seven by a neighbor, my response was to think I should have known better. By the time I was twenty-five, I was certain that I should have known better.

But I didn't at the time. I trusted this therapist. But I don't blame myself anymore. I can know I was taken advantage of and let go of the guilt. I know that a very sick person pulled me into a bad situation.

It was my anger that helped me through all of this. If I had simply stayed in the position of being hurt, I'm sure I wouldn't have had the strength to make the positive decisions I made.

I've learned that in some cases anger can be a friend.

THE LOSS OF A DREAM

Like every expectant father, I had dreams of what life would be like with a son. When the amniocentesis showed that this child was to be a boy, those dreams crystallized. It was easy to visualize us out in the sun, playing baseball on a breezy spring day, or walking along a manicured golf course on a Saturday morning. To me dreams like this were reality waiting to happen.

In expectation, my wife and I had created a Florida lifestyle. We traveled extensively and knew that this little boy was going to change a lot of that. We purchased a beach home, and again a dream was established. Long walks on the beach and playing in the sand became a part of the anticipated picture.

When our son was born, his spleen was four times normal size. During the first days of his life, his platelet count fell to below nine thousand. If he had started to bleed for any reason, it could have been fatal. The doctors agonized over the problem. I found myself confused and angry. My wife had done everything right! She'd followed all the nutritional recommendations and had prenatal care. Why was this happening? I saw a crack-addicted mother holding her healthy child. I screamed on the inside, *This is not fair!* What law of God would cause a thing like this to happen?

The Mayo Clinic finally confirmed a diagnosis—congenital erythropoietic porphyriah, a disorder that does not properly allow for the breakdown of porphyrins in the body. Porphyrins accumulate and are photosensitive chemicals. Our son could not be exposed to direct sunlight.

So many emotions raged through my mind. I felt guilty. Could it have somehow been my fault? I felt angry because I could not understand why. I felt sad as I projected onto my son how I thought he might feel in a few years. I felt lost. What would we do together? There would be no baseball, no sand castles at the beach and no birdie putts.

Over time I talked with many people. Of all of them, Tom Iverson comes to mind. He gave me the best advice I have never paid for. He said, "Pay attention and that child will teach you everything you need to know." Sure enough, he was right. I have stopped projecting my dreams onto my son. I'm trying to allow him to make his own dreams come true. I just want to be a part of them. He is the first thing in my life I realize I never want to live without.

This weekend my boy played for the Orlando Youth Hockey League Maple Leafs. They had two play-off games. In the stands I stood with a smile on my face. I'm a hockey dad. We now share ice hockey dreams.

Some Questions

What is it like to see to the heart of the matter;
Right through the skin and clear to the bone?
No disguises.
No back door.
No saved by the bell.
No God thrusting his hand through the ceiling
and pulling you to safety.

When all your thoughts hit;
When all your dreams fly loose;
When the anger locked away finally
Wakes up.

Will you have the strength to stand?
Or slam the shell closed again?

—Bill Chickering

PATIENCE

My father is a patient man. You have to be when you coach little-league baseball. Just imagine fifteen eight-year-olds (and their parents) with attitudes. What makes it even more exasperating is that your own son is the hardest to coach of all.

Every team needed a local sponsor, and our team stood out from all the rest. Car dealerships, a big furniture store and a couple of swanky restaurants sponsored the other teams. Not us. There we were, just a few years out of diapers, scampering around the field in uniforms with big red letters that proudly announced "Tiny's Package Store." That probably wouldn't happen today because there would be howls of indignation from well-meaning churches and recovery groups.

I was only eight, but I was already pretty stubborn. Though I was great with the glove in the field, hitting eluded me. I'd see other kids whacking hard grounders and fly balls and line drives. I'd either strike out or dribble a slow ground ball to the pitcher. My fielding average was about .990, and my batting average was .000.

That entire season, my father patiently tried to teach me how to stand in the batter's box—feet slightly spread apart and even with one another. Every time he tried to show me, I'd get angry and walk away. All Dad could do was shake his head and watch while I put my back foot at about a forty-five-degree angle to my front foot, also known as putting your foot "in the bucket."

Why did I do this? Because it felt comfortable to me. It just felt as though I could hit better when I stood that way.

I once heard a motivational speaker say, "If nothing changes, then nothing changes." That's the way it was with me. I kept my foot in the bucket, and my average stayed at .000. Any attempt to correct me was met with anger and an even more stubborn resolve.

Finally, however, I had had enough; I decided I'd do it my dad's way. It was the day of the all-star game (I got voted in because of my fielding, I guess). As I stepped in for my first at bat, I slowly placed my feet into the very awkward and unfamiliar stance my father had taught me.

I felt as though I'd fall over, but I kept the stance. The first pitch came in, but I had no intention of moving my bat at all. It was called a strike. The second pitch went outside. I thought of swinging but kept the bat snugly on my shoulder.

The third pitch came in about shoulder high and just a bit inside. I swung. I stood at home plate for a couple of seconds as the line drive cleared the third baseman's head and sailed out into left field. As I headed for second base in disbelief, I saw the ball scoot past the outstretched glove of the outfielder.

And although I didn't have to, I slid into home plate. The next thing I heard was people cheering and clapping. My teammates came out of the dugout and slapped me on the back. My dad grinned from ear to ear. He patted me on the back and said, "Way to go, Willie!"

My feet never again strayed from their appointed spot. The following year, I hit .250.; the year after that .340.

But I'll always remember how angry I got whenever my father tried to change my batting stance. I'd yell and kick the dirt and whine a lot—all because I didn't want to change. I knew my way was best, ignoring the fact that it wasn't productive and didn't bring any lasting satisfaction.

I wince when I think of how much my stubbornness and anger have cost me over the years. I think of how many times I flew off the handle, got angry and ignored the wisdom someone had to offer simply because I wouldn't consider any other way but my way.

Why do we get angry when people offer constructive help or advice? Why do we get upset when someone suggests it might be easier for us if we worked on changing a few behavior patterns?

Why? There are two reasons. First, we all have a healthy amount of pride and ego. If we listened to advice and things did improve, we might have to admit that our way wasn't best. That's hard to accept.

The second is trust. We may have learned from some harsh experience that not everyone who offered us advice had our best interests at heart. They may have offered help, then abandoned us, or may have exploited our vulnerability.

We take a risk when we trust anyone. That's just a fact of life. I still put my foot in the bucket from time to time, afraid to trust because I might have to shed a bit of my ego, or maybe even get hurt. But every once in a while, I hit that home run again and realize that though it's often risky, trust is worth the effort.

Like the Poet . . .

When the sadness and the anger subside,
I look for solace in the rhymes of others;
Words that sing and dance,
make noise and sparkle,
twirl and turn on the page so well
that I can dip my foot in the cold,
racing river,
brush away the silent
winter snow from my beard,
and angle that high pound test
deep into the brain;
where I can close my eyes and just fly
blind

—BILL CHICKERING

FAYE'S STORY

I'm still learning what it's like to work on the anger in my life. As I look back over the years, I can see many times when there were things I was angry about; but it was anger I never expressed. For the most part, I turned things inward. Or else I would turn to lots of work, or to alcohol, to get some relief from what I was feeling inside. It's always been difficult, as far as anger is concerned, to let out what I feel on the inside.

My husband was still in college when we got married. We lived in student housing. When he graduated, we moved east. He had a job that forced him to travel quite a bit. So I stayed home with the kids; we had four of them. The kids were sick a lot with the usual childhood kinds of things, and it kept me busy all the time.

I was resentful of the fact that my husband got to travel, and because of that, I thought about getting a divorce, though not seriously. And we were always short of money. That is difficult, too, especially when kids are involved. I remember one time when the money was tight. I was watching the news on television and saw my husband at a lavish banquet in New York. He would call me at home during the intermission of a Broadway play. That was hard for me, and only contributed to my anger and resentment at my situation.

What added to all the difficulty during these years was that my husband and I drank, and it was becoming a problem for both of us. I still thought about divorce. I just wanted to take the kids and move back to the Midwest, where I was comfortable and felt at home.

Well, it turned out that my husband also wanted to move back to the Midwest. He wanted to leave his job at a growing and successful company and start his own business. I was angry and resentful about this, too, because the company he worked for was advancing rapidly and eventually ended up instituting a great profit-sharing program for all its employees.

I had no idea how we would start a business since our money situation was still tight. My husband suggested that we approach Max and Irene, two close friends of mine who were quite wealthy, and ask them for the money to get started.

This was difficult because Max and Irene were like surrogate parents to me. They had known me most of my life. Irene was a major influence in my life; she helped me gain self-esteem and let me know that I was worth something. Both she and Max were very, very special to me.

So it angered me that my husband wanted to go to them for money because I swore I would never do that—I felt that would be taking advantage of their friendship. But my husband did ask them, and Max interceded for us and called a bank. We ended up getting the loan that helped us open a hardware store. What we didn't know was that the bank had also backed another hardware store and that we just couldn't compete.

Our store wasn't doing well. We were borrowing more and more money, and our alcoholism just got worse and worse. Things headed downhill fast. Max and Irene wanted me to leave my husband, and they wanted to hire someone else to run the hardware business. The arguments between us became intense, and we threw a lot of anger around.

Max died not long after that, and I blamed my husband for

what happened. And although I had known Max as a father for years, I felt humiliated by everything that had happened and didn't go to his funeral. Max's son eventually called and told me that they were going to put the store up for auction. The auction didn't bring much, however.

The stress took its toll on my husband. He found another job, but the pressure and the business failure had been just too much for him to handle. One morning, he woke up and said he couldn't decide what socks to put on. Shortly thereafter, he ended up in a psychiatric ward.

So I had to take care of everything—the kids, creditors pounding at the door, my husband and the humiliation of it all. One day, I went to our local grocery store, where I had always had credit, and in front of my friends and acquaintances, the grocer told me my credit was no longer good there.

Through all of this our drinking escalated. Events seemed to spiral out of control. My husband suffered a heart attack. The IRS attached our assets. My husband and I divorced. And then last, but certainly not least, my husband and I confronted our alcoholism. We participated in a treatment program and then began long-term recovery. Eventually, we managed to become friends.

I had a rather idealistic view of what my recovery would mean. I thought that once I was clean and sober, my troubles would vanish and all of life's circumstances would change for the better.

God quickly corrected that false notion. Just five days after I got out of treatment, my mother died. Three months later I was hit by a drunk driver and nearly killed. One thing I did listen to in treatment, however, was not to make any hasty, drastic changes or decisions in my life. Since one of my children was only two years away from high school graduation, I decided to maintain the status quo until then. I ran a small accounting business and kept things financially intact with that.

One day that all changed. My daughter called and told me that doctors suspected she had ovarian cancer and that she was going in for some tests. When she went in for surgery, the doctors opened her up, saw the extent of the cancer, and then closed. She was told she had about two months to live. I closed my business and went to work for my son.

There's no expressing the loss you feel when your child dies—it's a feeling even beyond grief. I lay beside my daughter and held her close as she died. She'd asked me to promise her to do that, and so I did. She also told me to promise that I would enroll in a counselor training program. I did that as well, and I'm grateful to my son for providing me with the means and the support to do that.

But with all that had happened, I was numb. All I could think was *I have to keep going. I can't stop. I have to keep going.* I never allowed myself to feel much anger. I've felt it in bits and spurts, but to this day, I still don't think I've allowed much of it to get out.

Two months after I started training, my ex-husband died. That was one time I do remember feeling real anger, anger at my husband and anger at God. I was mad at my husband because he would get to be with our daughter. For the first time in my life, I thought of suicide, but something inside me would not let me quit. I do not know what kept me going. All I felt was, *God, I cannot go and pick out another casket. I just cannot do it.* But instead of talking about it or getting angry about it, I just closed off and sealed another compartment inside me.

I can only think of one time when I really let it all out. It was right at the beginning of my daughter's illness. I ran away, just took off, right after a major fight with my son and daughter-in-law. I got in my car and started driving, down through the southern part of Minnesota and into Iowa, where in the midst of threatening, tornado-like weather, I pulled into a small motel. I screamed at God. All I remember saying is, "Give me a goddamn sign! Just give me a goddamn sign!"

I had been gone for three days, and everyone was looking for me. My daughter told me that she had not been worried, that she had known God and I needed to spend some time alone.

But I felt guilty. I felt I didn't have the right to act out my anger, so I turned things inward again.

There have been times over the years when I have burst out at family members and others, and then felt guilty and turned inward again. I've just never given myself the luxury of doing this. I always thought that after all I'd been through, there would be some kind of reward waiting for me, and I thought that if I acted out my anger, I would destroy whatever reward was coming.

And while I still feel that way, things are slowly changing. I'm doing a lot more writing in areas that I like and working in a field where I know I can give some help to a lot of people. For the first time in my life, I feel that it may be okay to have some fun.

THE NIGHT OF STARS

For anyone who has ever experienced a prolonged siege of depression, or for any family member who has alternately supported and stood hopelessly by a loved one, bumper sticker psychology and fawning bromides about "God's will" and "Think positive" ring hollow. They usually evoke an immediate and angry response since most of the time they come from people who've never been through the crippling consequences of depression or known its all-consuming force. It's almost best, I think, that well-meaning people forgo conversation and simply sit quietly and listen for a while. At times, I feel that far beyond the basic human needs of food, water, air and touch, the need to give advice, even when struck mute, seems to surpass them all.

I speak as someone who has lived both sides of the coin. Years ago, for a period of about two months, I went through a depression so black that it nearly paralyzed me. It was not something that came upon me gradually. I woke up one morning, and it was simply there—unannounced and deeply embedded.

In retrospect, I'm a lot clearer now as to what might have brought the depression on. For nearly twenty years, I had ferociously abused alcohol. If one drink worked, then seven would work even better. Through the help of some friends and a diligent and compassionate AA sponsor, I quit drinking.

I became depressed about ten months after I sobered up. What I'd experienced, I discovered, was not uncommon among recovering alcoholics. I'd used the alcohol to medicate, to calm the storm inside me. Now I was sober, with no place to hide the rage, the fear and the anger. So I turned it inward. The stories that I heard from other alcoholics gave me hope, and even made me laugh from time to time. A few of the old-time AA members told me, "You're right on schedule."

But it did pass.

When someone you love or someone close to you goes through severe depression, whether it's just an episode or a life-long battle spotted here and there with periods of relief, you can feel just as helpless as if you were going through it yourself.

The depression may come quickly or else wedge its way in over time. For people who are on antidepressant medication, that medication can suddenly stop working. The person who is suffering may not even know the medication's quit. Instead, they may begin finding behaviors to cope, whether it's to isolate, go on a strict diet, become compulsively neat or a host of other behaviors.

Eventually, however, the moment comes when all the coping mechanisms and defenses fail. Then the real battle begins. Doctor visits, hospital stays, and a long regimen of trial and error with new medications may await.

So you stand back and watch someone who was once full of life now slowed to almost a crawl. And you drift through all the well-known stages of grief—denial, anger, bargaining and, finally, acceptance.

Then you begin to blame yourself: *Why didn't I see it coming? I should have known. Was it something I did that set it off?* Quit. You didn't cause it. And only time, and in some cases medication, can calm the anguish.

There are a number of self-help books on depression. All of them contain gems of wisdom and counsel that you can pluck and keep as your own.

The best help I found, however, was an eighty-five-page book—a personal memoir entitled *Darkness Visible,* by William

Styron, the author of such classic novels as *Sophie's Choice, Lie Down in Darkness* and *The Confessions of Nat Turner.*

The author vividly recounts the details of his six-month journey into a suicidal depression that ended up hospitalizing him for nearly two months. He recalls the illness's first vague twitching and the evening when he took his personal journal, tied it neatly and carefully wrapped it, as you would a parcel for mailing. He threw the journal in the trash. He had planned to kill himself but instead wound up in the hospital.

Styron offers sound advice for family members and friends of people who fall prey to depression. More than anything else, he says, be encouraging, constantly encouraging, even if you feel foolish: "A tough job this; calling 'Chin up!' from the safety of the shore to a drowning person is tantamount to insult, but it has been shown over and over again that if the encouragement is dogged enough—and the support equally committed and passionate—the endangered one can nearly always be saved."

The author gives the reader the gift of hope. He recalls Dante's epic poem *The Inferno,* an account of the author's journey deep into the levels of hell and darkness. He asks us to remember the journey, but also one of the final lines *"E quindi uscimmo a riveder le stelle."* ("And so we came forth and once again beheld the stars.")

And it will pass.

A HANDFUL OF DUST

This book started out as project, a contract signed and an obligation to fulfill. My cowriter and I would divide the book up into sections and gather stories from everyday people who had experienced loss and anger. Around those stories, we would write some short essays, attempting to focus the point of certain sections and bring it home for the reader. Our goal was to put together a book in which somewhere, in one or more of the stories, readers could see their own experiences and gain a measure of hope. It was information gathering. It was research.

But then it got personal. It came to live in my spirit and forced me to pay heed to what was going on inside.

My wife had worked in a profession she loved for more than twelve years, a helping profession. Each day, she and those around her counseled others and gave of themselves. The pay would never make her rich, but the money is not why she chose her line of work. Over the years, dozens and dozens of people have written her, called her or talked to her personally and thanked her for the difference she made in their lives. I recall with a deep sense of pride a reunion dinner she attended several years ago. Person after person came up to her, hugged her and thanked her. Their lives had turned around. She had given them the push they needed to overcome the problems, hurts and personal pain, and get back into the world and start living again.

About three years ago, my wife and I relocated to another state. She had accepted another position within her company at one of their satellite facilities. We had heard some troubling stories about where we were headed—about people breaking down emotionally and physically from the stress. But we were newly married, up for the challenge of something new, and our initial impression had actually been pretty good. So off we went, believing we were invincible.

Once we arrived, however, things changed; and they changed quickly—for both of us, but for my wife especially. The first war we fought together was over money. Everyone in the organization received a bonus that year. We thought that was great because the extra money would come in handy. Then my wife was told she wouldn't get the bonus because even though she was a ten-year employee, she hadn't worked at her new position long enough and was therefore ineligible for a bonus. When she pointed out that the bonus was company-wide, she was told the answer was still no. It was only when someone intervened on her behalf that the money came through.

And it went downhill from there. My wife lived on a steady diet of verbal blastings, half-truths and broken promises. She built a solid team of competent people and dearly valued them and their efforts. There were also several wonderful folks who supported her, showing her care and concern amidst their own trials and frustrations. In addition, there were people within the parent organization who lent their support and understanding long-distance, and one person in particular who was simply a saint. And though my wife tried to run her end of the organization as best she could, each day when she came home, I could see she had died just a little bit more.

I could go on, but I'll stop here. The bottom line is this—two and half years into the job, I admitted her to the hospital with cardiac problems, infections, and rapidly rising and falling blood-sugar levels. She could barely stand up because her legs shook every time she tried to walk, and she was in tears for hours at a time. The doctors who treated her were not strangers to her illness. They, and others who helped, all asked the same question: "What the hell is going on over there?"

My visit to the hospital shook me deeply. The beautiful, vibrant, caring woman I had married was a shell, just trying to hold on while her body stabilized.

Yet it still wasn't over. In the midst of all this, we got a call from her job saying that the bonus she had earned the previous year was being withheld because she had missed a required employee meeting while she was on medical leave. She would get the money, but only when she returned to work and signed a paper saying she had watched a video of the meeting she had missed. It took the threat of outside action to get the check.

One day, upon returning from a visit to the hospital, my anger was past the point of rage. It was going to take my wife a long time to recover; but she's a fighter and a survivor, and I knew that she would.

I had to ask myself some hard questions. We've spread a little advice in this book, advice I hold to with conviction. But when it came down to this, I realized how hard it was to put into practice what I believe in principle. Then, my gut feeling was pretty basic: Someone is going to pay for this, and they're going to pay dearly. I wanted to step on someone and watch the person squirm.

But I also recalled a biblical teaching, and I wondered whether that might be the best way to go. In the New Testament gospels, Christ sends pairs of his disciples out into the countryside to preach in the towns and stay in the homes of people along the way. He instructs them that if they're turned away and treated disrespectfully and inhospitably, they're not to return the same. They're told instead to shake the dust from their feet as they depart. It's a nonviolent ritual that sends others a simple message: Expect nothing here; do not waste your time. The gesture both expresses anger and hostility, and says, "It's time to move on."

Now if you'll pardon me, I've got to round up some dust.

Steps

You can see the beginning of the journey,
And where the first step leads;
Leads away from the rudder, away
from the wheel,
away from the throttle.

The journey does not begin with a push, but
just a step;
Stepping back from your anger and looking
at it carefully,
Stepping back from what you cannot control
and letting it be.

Watch it all whirl or watch
it all stand still;
Watch it do whatever it wishes to do.
Why, even your own growth takes place
at a pace you do not dictate.

Now just stand back;
Roses will bloom,
The skies will rain and snow;
People will be born and
People will die.
And it will all happen whether you
Lock up inside, or whether
You let it go.

Just stand back.

—BILL CHICKERING

SECTION TWO CLOSE: HEALING NEVER ENDS

Out of perfection nothing can be made.
Every process involves breaking something up.

—Joseph Campbell

You have to sift the dirt to find the gold, but that's not enough. The gold must go through the refinement of fire to filter out the impurities that were missed the first time through. Still, however, you never quite get it all.

In the Bible, Saint Paul warns us that it is dangerous to think that you ever arrive, or finally get there, or have it all together. I'm sure we all have met individuals who believe they are at the arrival point; rather pleasant folks to be around, aren't they?

We can do the same thing when it comes to setting goals in our life. We can say to ourselves, *If I could only get to that spot, I'd have it made. I wouldn't want anything more.* It reminds us of a story we heard about a young man who had dreams of becoming a top-flight editor, who worked hard and saw it paying off. He and a colleague, who both labored at a small publishing house for very little money, always told themselves, *Man, wouldn't it be great if we could edit books for* that *publishing company?* This young man went even further and often said to himself, *If I got to edit for* that *publishing company, I would have arrived. I wouldn't want anything else.*

Several years later this young man was freelancing, when one day he got a call from *that* publishing company asking him to fly in and pick up a manuscript from the editor-in-chief. Our friend flew in and met with the editor. It was a quick meeting— the instructions were clear and succinct. He wanted to celebrate. He had a couple of hours before his flight, so he headed for the airport lounge for a couple of drinks. He sat back in a comfortable chair, got ready to sip his drink, when it hit him like a hammer blow to the face: *My God, this is it. This is what I always wanted. But wait a second. I'm only thirty. I want to do a lot more with my life. This can't be it.*

Our friend saw the folly of dreaming of perfection. But even more than that, he now understood that to cut the process short meant cutting into his dreams and plans and future goals. Each accomplishment, he realized, was only a step on the road to more learning and self-discovery, even if that discovery took him over some bumpy roads at times.

Campbell's statement helps us understand two things. First, you can't do anything with perfection—nothing. You can't work on it; you can't make it better. Second, you must trust the process, even if it involves busting up some old habit patterns and some old ways of thinking.

Abraham Maslow designed what has been described as the Maslow hierarchy of needs. At the top of this hierarchy is self-actualization. In a way, self-actualization is to have "arrived." What would you do if you were truly self-actualized? We suspect it would be rather boring. There would probably be no one to talk to. You would possibly be all alone.

The reality is that life is a fleeting process. Some moments we feel we've nearly arrived; other times we feel thousands of miles from our destination.

In this section, "Deeper Hurts," the reader has been introduced to people who are lost. These people tried so many ways to make their anger and pain go away. Some used alcohol and drugs. Some just stuffed it. Others exploded and externalized their rage. Internalized anger led others to contemplate suicide. For these people, positive change seemed remote.

A consistent theme throughout this section involved a process called grief. The operative word is *process*. It takes place over a period of time. For some people, it takes a relatively short period of time; for others, it seems to take a lifetime, and even then it's never totally resolved. The past does not go away. You can grieve a hurt or a loss; but even when acceptance and coping are established, history is still history. In this section there have been discussions of the various stages of the grief process. These stages range from shock to anger to denial and, ultimately, to bargaining, depression and acceptance. Anger, in many ways, has been viewed as a critical step along the way. In some cases it is a necessary element in the journey toward personal enlightenment.

In this section there are two basic grief themes that evolve. The first theme involves individuals who suffered hurt and loss later in their life. An example is the story of John T. John suffered the loss of his best friend. He was a college student who had developed certain coping skills that helped him deal with the acute loss. The second type of scenario involves a deeper, more developmental hurt. Here we read stories of very young people who were hurt at times in their lives when they were solely dependent on parents and other role models. Maybe the greatest hurt of all is the hurt received at the hands of those that you should be able to trust. The story of John W. is an example of such hurt. His relationship with his father is painful to read about. In the chapter "Lessons," the story of Diane also is an example of hurt inflicted on someone at a developmental age, when a person does not have the experience and coping skills to tolerate such abuse.

The types of hurt and anger that we have read about in this section are not easy to heal. What can they do? There are certainly no easy answers. But we will try to define them.

Later Life Trauma: In John T.'s case, the reader views a man who's lost his closest friend. Adults endure many types of loss. Loss of family, divorce, loss of job, car wrecks with resulting injury, a diagnosis of chronic illness and the loss of a child are just a few examples. Although John is in his twenties, the important thing to remember is that he is old enough to have established some coping skills. What is most helpful to him is the support and understanding of those around him.

People undergoing a posttraumatic or acute stress reaction may exhibit certain symptoms. These symptoms are of three types:

1. **Hyperarousal:** Individuals experiencing hyperarousal symptoms will be hypersensitive to feelings. They will appear edgy, as if nervously waiting for another traumatic event to occur. They often have difficulty concentrating and sleep poorly.

2. **Intrusion:** Intrusion is the involuntary reexperiencing of the traumatic event. Symptoms include intrusive memories, nightmares or even flashbacks.

3. **Constriction:** After a period of hyperarousal and involuntary reexperiencing of the event, the brain seems to get tired, and it can actually shut down. Constriction consists of avoiding feelings, thoughts and situations reminiscent of the trauma.

Often the individuals may feel as if they are losing their mind. Many of the symptoms described above occur in numerous psychiatric disorders. It's important that the individuals understand they are *not* losing their mind or going crazy. In essence, they're having a normal reaction to an abnormal situation. The problem is that this reaction may be interfering with their life and hurting their relationships with others. If the symptoms are so severe that they are interfering with work, family and personal functions, then professional help is needed. A psychiatrist, a psychologist or other therapist who understands grief and trauma can be particularly helpful in allowing these individuals to talk through, fully understand and develop appropriate coping mechanisms to handle the symptoms.

For those individuals whose symptoms are not so severe, "here and now" strategies can be utilized. These strategies are a combination of cognitive and behavioral approaches that can help stabilize you. For example, a three-by-five index card can be used to develop a safety plan. On the index card, write down four things you can do that will help if you start experiencing symptoms such as dreams, irritability or difficulty concentrating. These strategies should include someone you can call and other behaviors that you find to be soothing. For example, one strategy could be to call a friend. Another might be to read from the Bible. A third might be to take a long walk. A fourth strategy could involve the use of deep-breathing exercises. The number of approaches is unlimited, and the strategies are based on what works for you. A second strategy is to keep a journal, and record a list of all the symptoms you are experiencing as well as any other written dialogue that expresses your feelings and thoughts as you move through the grief process.

The best way to understand the symptom list is by listening

to the following stories. Have you ever come home and noticed that the house was a mess and said to yourself, *I really just want to sit in front of the TV set.* But by force of will you moved yourself to clean up the house. You didn't seem to have the energy at first, but you noticed as you completed the task that your energy level was greater, and you felt better about yourself and more in control of your life. Another example involves going to work and noticing that there were so many things to do that you felt overwhelmed. If you sat down and wrote a "to do" list and prioritized the tasks, it seemed to give a feeling of control. In the same way, keeping a symptom list allows those going through a grief process to feel more in control of what's going on in their life.

Another technique might be to purchase a small notebook and every time you experience a symptom, to sit down and act like a newspaper reporter. Write down where you were, whom you were with, what time of day it was and any other pertinent details. This strategy forces you to use the cognitive part of your brain instead of the more emotional center. It serves as an eloquent little intervention to help center you.

The symptoms of grief can last for days, weeks, months or years. Usually, with time, the symptoms will diminish. There may be times when you will recall the event. This can be triggered by being in the same vicinity or around anyone that reminds you of the painful experience.

In John T.'s case, we saw a healthy young man who was able to find strength in the support around him, although that strength and support came from places that he could not have imagined. In the following scenarios we'll see a different type of grief, one that is more deep-seated. This kind of hurt can be described as sanctuary trauma. This is trauma that occurs at the hands of those you should be able to love and trust. It is deeper and more painful and much more difficult to cope with.

Deeper Developmental Hurt: How do you work through hurt that is deep and occurred at a very early age? The hurt occurred at a time when you had neither the coping skills nor the support system to adequately help you deal with the trauma. What if the support system is the perpetrator? That is the situation in the cases of John W. and Diane. You read about John being abused and betrayed by those around him. Diane's case involved early incest and what is often called repetition compulsion. The hurt keeps repeating itself throughout her life. These traumas are more difficult to understand and much more emotional. The reader will notice a stronger reaction to this type of trauma, a reaction often involving anger and at times, disbelief.

Anything that triggers that old situation often creates within the individual feelings of anger and fear. The old situations are still looked at through the eyes of a six- or seven-year-old. They are looked at through the eyes of the individual at the age of the original trauma. I'll give you an example. I once worked with a twenty-nine-year-old female who suffered from what at the time was referred to as "frigidity." She was very attractive but had no history of sexual relationships. She worked in the basement of a hospital, filing charts. One Saturday, the medical records department of that hospital went to a movie as a departmental outing. During the movie, a young man sat next to Barbara. He reached over and tried to hold her hand, and as he did so, she broke his nose. When she came into my office the next day, she said to me, after retelling the story, "This is not normal, is it?" In fact, this woman was an incest survivor, who was abused by her older brother. The reader can remember the discussions throughout this section of the old developmental themes. The developmental theme of sexuality plays out here.

This deeper type of hurt causes a more complicated post-trauma reaction. Often this reaction can be perceived in three ways. The first of these ways involves physiological changes that occur inside of the individual. Trauma can actually cause physical changes. As a matter of fact, Sigmund Freud's original conception of hysteria was theorized to have been caused by incest. Today, a lot of what is described as psychosomatic illness involves individuals with early repeated life-trauma. There are biological changes, which occur secondary to this trauma, that can mimic anxiety and depression. There are abnormalities of the endogenous opioid system that leave the individual vulnerable to pain and anxiety. These individuals actually like crises because they cause a release of endorphins and enkephalins that act as opium-like substances within the body, allowing them to feel calm. These individuals can also experience sleep abnormalities and numerous gastrointestinal symptoms. For example, one study showed that 60 percent of individuals diagnosed with irritable-bowel syndrome had a history of incest. Such maladies as migraine headaches are also common. A second area of disturbance involves personal identity and relationships. People who are hurt or abused early in life have problems with personal boundaries. They do not have a solidified sense of self. Difficulties in interpersonal relationships might be seen. These individuals also tend to exhibit many impulsive disturbances. For example, they may cut or burn themselves and often have hidden eating disorders. The third area of disturbance involves consciousness. This may be better referred to as dissociation. An individual may have learned to check out when under stress. It's easy to imagine that a six-year-old who is undergoing sexual abuse might actually dissociate from his or her body as a way to survive. The problem is that later in life when this individual is in a stressful situation in a relationship, on the job or while trying to raise children, the same tendency will come to the fore. This person will dissociate and often be unable to remember the dialogue or the commitments made while in the dissociate state.

In the stories of John W. and Diane, the reader will remember that they required more then just support and understanding. Their journeys involved professional help. It's also important to recall that their journeys had no definitive endings. What had happened to them will always be with them. The goal is to reduce the symptoms and to allow a more objective understanding as opposed to viewing certain life events through childlike eyes. Professional help is often called for in order to promote such a change.

Survivors of deep developmental hurt have distorted views of the world. To them the world is not a place where there are some people you can trust. To the survivor the world is a place you cannot trust. The relationship with a therapist can help individuals to see the world as a better place and to make better choices within their world. Some form of insight-oriented therapy (i.e., looking back at what happened in their life and gaining some understanding) can diminish the intensity of the symptoms described above. Sometimes these individuals need medication as well as therapy. Often psychiatric referral can be helpful. The bottom line here is that the trauma is so deep that it's not easily worked through.

When searching for a therapist, the individual should call a number of therapists and ask friends who have also seen a therapist. Shop for a therapist just as you would for a new car. Find the names that continuously pop up as being competent and then choose from those clinicians.

To close this section, we're reminded of an individual who described growing up in a house where there was constant yelling and sporadic violence. The home situation was totally unpredictable and chaotic. He said that he remembered being five years old and sitting in the dark in an upstairs bedroom. His three-year-old sister was with him. He remembers them sitting in total darkness with only their legs touching. Downstairs the mother and father were screaming at each other, using profanity and threatening words. The individual says today that every time he's around anger, he wants to go back to that dark bedroom, where it is safe and no one can find him. In section two, this is the type of experience that is common to so many who have undergone deeper hurts. These old hurts don't go away; they don't easily pass. Anything that brings back the old memories can often trigger the old experience. However, as we've seen here, there are degrees. For some, it's a simple moving through, aided by those who love and care for them. For others, their whole life seems to be in upheaval. They never completely work through the old hurt that is constantly lurking in the background, influencing their every move and decision.

Epilogue

It almost seems to be a human instinct to desire formulas that will totally relieve us of uncertainty and the necessity to agonize over important decisions.

—M. Scott Peck, M.D.
Denial of the Soul

We think life should be like a symphony, ordered and neat, in harmonious, measurable sections. It should start with a theme, rise to a crescendo, play through a moderately softer version of the theme, then build to a stunning and resolute climax—theme completed, triumph.

But perhaps life is more like jazz, improvisational and often wandering—instrumental solos that drift off to no place in particular and musicians who simply stop playing when they feel like it, not when they're supposed to.

Legendary trumpeter Miles Davis would play around with the horn, blow a few notes, then point to an unsuspecting member of his quartet as if to say, "You pick it up from here." When it was time for him to do a solo, he'd turn his back on the audience and not seem to give a damn whether anyone approved or not. It was almost a bit mad, this routine of his.

Yet it was satisfying. Miles would often look back at the audience with a rather puzzled smirk on his face that seemed to say, "You want direction? Go read a map."

We do want a map, don't we? We want to know where the turns are, how fast to go, where the rest stops are located and what roads are under construction. We want a book, a speaker, a guru, a tape, a guide—someone, anyone who will tell us what we're supposed to do next. Whether it's our relationships, our sexuality, our emotions, nutrition or exercise equipment, we want something to take away our choice, something to decide for us.

That's why M. Scott Peck's writings are so pertinent. It's also the reason *The Road Less Traveled* was on the bestsellers list for more than six hundred weeks. Why? Because it said what we wanted to say, but didn't know how. It said "Life is messy and sloppy and won't always fall into place for you. Here are some things you might consider doing with your life, but don't be surprised if you still struggle. Don't be surprised if you fail. There are no guarantees."

We ate it up because it spoke the truth.

Aside from a simple belief in the destination, there is another common component we all possess—faith. Some of us trust God. Some of us trust the process of life. Others aren't too sure what to trust but keep working and keep traveling nonetheless.

Trust implies living with the unknown and being comfortable with it. It implies walking forward when we don't know what the next stop may bring. It implies making a decision before all the facts are in and all the scales balanced. It implies loving in the face of great hardship and turmoil, and a willingness to forgive.

We all have the tools to deal with our anger; we all have the tools with which to heal. What often keeps us from using those tools, however, is the depth of our hurt and sorrow or that of someone we love. The anger may go so deep that it renders us speechless and powerless. There are people, or things, or institutions, or even God, whom we want to get back at, whom we want to hurt and show just how it feels.

And we can't. Somebody should pay, but they probably won't. We want to trust in "karma," that what goes around comes around; but that takes too long. We know we can't stay in a place of rage and helplessness too long. We'd probably go crazy. It's at our point of deepest frustration, however, that we often find our deepest reservoir of strength, wisdom and sanity. At some point in the fight, we come to understand that the best thing we can do is move on and begin to rebuild our own lives. We may even, at these points of ultimate frustration, have fleeting thoughts of forgiveness cross our mind—just fleeting, mind you. When those feelings hit, it may feel to us like we've weakened or softened, or begun to give up the fight.

The hurt and the pain may still be with us for a long time, and the anger may still rise when we recall the past. But something in us—we may not even know what or why—has told us that we've spent long enough, that even through the most painful of sufferings there comes a point at which holding on to the anger becomes more painful than what we were angry about.

Our road map is often blurred, and our directions are often unclear. And just as in jazz, we may wander off on solos and wonder just what tune it was that we were trying to play in the first place.

It may not always be comfortable and sweet. But it is beautiful music.

It is our hope that these stories have helped you to listen, understand and even appreciate the "music" within you.

We hope you've learned that although anger can be brutal, it can also be wise. Anger can maim, and anger can heal. Anger can be unfair, and it can be just. Anger can spur us to action, or it can stop us dead in our tracks. Anger can lift our self-esteem, or it can move us to self-pity or remorse. Anger can show us what is wrong with us and with our world, and it can alert us to what wrongs need to be set straight. Anger can be fair, and it can take sides. Anger can bring us to tears, and it can bring us to joy. Anger can make us lash out, or it can help us hold back.

If there is one thing we've learned from putting this book together, it is that we are certain to err if we assign a hard and fast moral judgment to anger. It simply can't be done. If anything, it is situational, seemingly very appropriate sometimes and completely out of line at other times.

We hope that the stories and reflections that you've read in this book have in some way helped you understand your anger and the role it plays for you day by day. And finally, we hope that you've in some way been comforted and assured by what you've read in these pages, and maybe even picked up a tip or two along the way that will make your own path a bit easier.

One must accept the ironies of life
and take up the tasks of life. Disgraced or
not, foolish or wise, living in ill times
or good, we are what we are, we are where
we are. The actual world is our
only world. We must go forward; we must
accept all that men say of us, however
painful or unfair it be. The times allow for
no delay. Life grants us no space for
idleness, regrets, the pursuit of illusions.
The work of peace must go on, in hardiness
and steadfast good humor. We must
consent to being ourselves, to being the
unworthy vessels of God's word, to working
with others, to the slow inching forward
of compassion and hope.

—Daniel Berrigan, S.J.
Consequences: Truth and . . .

Works Cited

Bergman, Susan. *Anonymity: The Secret Life of the American Family.* New York: Warner Books, 1994.

Berrigan, Daniel S.J. *Consequences: Truth and . . .* New York: Macmillan, 1967.

DiGuiseppe, Ray. "The Diagnosis, Assessment, and Treatment of Clients with Anger Problems" workshop. Presented at *U.S. Journal's* Counseling Skills for the New Millennium Conference, Charlotte, N.C., September 1997.

The Harvard Mental Health Letter. July 1997, Vol. 14, No. 1, pg. 3.

Jackson, Phil. *Sacred Hoops.* New York: Hyperion, 1995.

Johnson, Robert. *Owning Your Own Shadow.* San Francisco: Harper Collins, 1993.

Levine, Saul. "The Development of Wickedness—From Whence Does Evil Stem?" *Psychiatric Annals.* September 1997, pg. 617, Vol. 27, No. 9.

Moore, Thomas. *Care of the Soul.* New York: Harper Collins, 1992.

Noonan, Peggy. *Backward and Upward: The New Conservative Writing.* Edited by David Brooks. New York: Random House, 1996.

Peck, M. Scott. *Denial of the Soul.* New York: Harmony Books, 1997.

Rogers, Carl. *On Becoming a Person.* Boston: Houghton-Mifflin, Co., 1961.

Spence, Gerry. *How to Argue and Win Every Time.* New York: St. Martin's Press, 1995.

Styron, William. *Darkness Visible.* New York: Random House, Inc., 1990.

Wholey, Dennis. *Discovering Happiness.* New York: Avon Books, 1988.